The Liveaboard Report

A Boat Dweller's Guide to What Works and What Doesn't

Charlie Wing

International Marine
Camden, Maine

Published by International Marine®, an imprint of TAB Books. TAB
Books is a division of McGraw-Hill, Inc.

10 9 8 7 6 5 4 3

Library of Congress Cataloging-in-Publication Data

Wing, Charles, 1939–
The Liveaboard Report : a boat dweller's guide to what works and what
doesn't / Charlie Wing.
p. cm.
Includes index.
ISBN 0–87742– 378–4
1. Houseboats--Designs and construction. 2. Boat living--United States.
3. Boats and boating--Miscellanea. I. Title.
VM335.W55 1993
728.7'8--dc20   93-17644
                                                             CIP

Questions regarding the content of this book should be addressed to:
International Marine
P.O. Box 220
Camden, ME 04843

Questions regarding the ordering of this book should be addressed to:
TAB Books
A Division of McGraw-Hill, Inc.
Blue Ridge Summit, PA 17294
1-800-233-1128

The Liveaboard Report is printed on 60# Renew Opaque Vellum, an acid-
free paper that contains 50 percent recycled waste paper (preconsumer)
and 10 percent postconsumer waste paper.

Printed by R.R. Donelley, Harrisonburg, VA.

Contents

Acknowledgments

Without my mate, Judy, I would never have gone cruising. But giving up seventy-one interview afternoons, many cruises, and half of the precious living space of our home, *Puffin*, went beyond the call of duty.

I also have to give credit to our five cats: Cricket, Toshiyuki, Little Orphan Annie, Thai, and Festus. Many times they saved the manuscript from blowing overboard by napping on the loosely strewn papers, and, by walking across the keyboard, they would remind me to save my computer files.

Finally, there are the seventy-one crews who subjected themselves to my four-hour questionnaire. It is their experience and wisdom, not mine, upon which this book is based. I thank them for their time, their insight, and, in many cases, their continuing friendship.

Most books are the result of someone thinking they have something interesting to say. This book is just the opposite. Let me explain.

In my past life I had run a school for owner-builders, hosted a PBS series on remodeling, and written seven homebuilding books. Now I found myself living and cruising aboard a boat. I had to continue writing to support myself, but I had no further interest in houses. Worse, I knew next to nothing about boats—certainly too little to write a book about them. What was I to do?

Then I met Tom and Mary Ann Young from Vermont. Tom understood my dilemma. He was a builder by trade and a novice liveaboard like myself. He asked, "Why don't you write a book about what you don't know—all the things about living aboard that we need to know but haven't yet learned?"

What an idea! The next night the Wings and the Youngs met and compiled a list of 400 questions they'd like to ask more experienced cruisers. Over the following six months, I had the pleasure of asking those 400 questions of 71 crews I found underway in the Intracoastal Waterway and the Bahamas. This book is the compilation of their answers.

As such, this book is different from other cruising handbooks. This author is not saying, "Listen up, turkey—I am an expert, and this is *the* way to do it."

This author is saying, "I asked this question of 71 crews whose experience living aboard totalled 277 years and 106,000 nautical miles. Three percent said 'X,' 20% said 'Y,' and 77% said 'Z.' Let this be your guide."

I hope you find their advice as helpful as I have.

1. The Hull

I thought the broker said it was in perfect condition.

Introduction

Choosing a hull is like choosing the structure in which you will make your land-based home: large or small, one story or two, brick or wood, garage or no. The characteristics of your hull will have as great an effect on your lifestyle as on your speed through the water.

Do you want to roam afar or stay in one harbor? Do you enjoy fast and bouncy, or are you the slow and comfortable type? Are you a diehard sailor, or do you turn to the engine when your speed drops to five knots? Is wood your religion, or do you consider wood hulls a pain?

In this chapter cruisers share with you their feelings about hull type, size, material, and maturity.

What type of boat do you currently have?

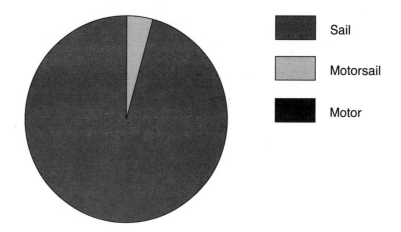

Motorboats are not included in the survey. Although the survey originally anticipated motorboats, the first motor-boat interview changed the rules.

Questioning the owner of a 42-foot motorboat in a marina, I asked for his estimated annual budget.

"About $13,000," he replied.

"That's about average for the annual budgets of the dozen or so sailboats I've interviewed," I said.

"Oh, no," he said. "That's our *monthly* budget!"

My decision then and there was that motorboats would be the subject of a separate survey.

What type of boat would you pick next time?

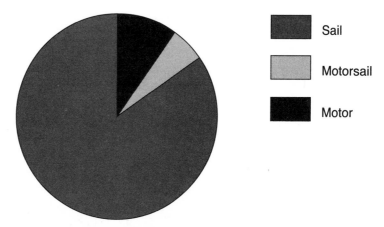

For their next boats, 10% would pick a motorboat and 3% a motorsailer. Many, however, speculated that their *final* boat might be a trawler.

The reason most often given for switching to power was the increasing difficulty of handling sails as one gets older.

What is the length on deck (LOD) of your current boat?

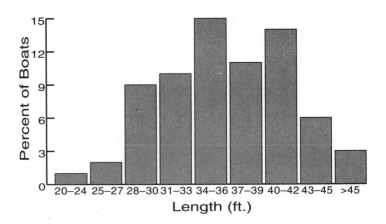

The overall average length on deck was exactly 37 feet.

The degree to which families of three or four, and even families with dogs, had adapted to a space of 30 by 8 feet is remarkable. Very few *complained* of their boats being too small, although given unlimited resources, most would elect to move up, as the numbers below demonstrate.

If cost were no object, what would be the length of your next boat?

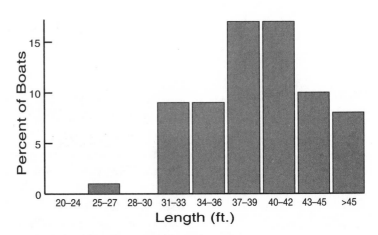

The average desired boat length, given unlimited resources, was 39 feet 8 inches.

Of 28 boats under 35 feet, 24 owners wished for a larger boat. Of 20 current boats between 40 and 45 feet, six desired smaller, five larger, and nine the same. Significantly, *all* owners of current boats over 45 feet desired smaller boats. At the other end, the single boater desiring a length of 25 to 27 feet was a confirmed singlehander.

Of what material is your current hull constructed?

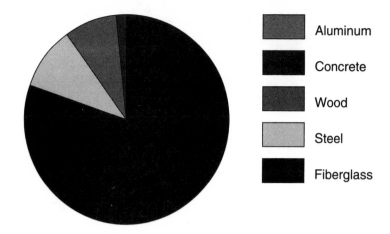

Eighty percent of the hulls were of fiberglass, 10% steel, 9% wood, and 1% ferrocement. There were no aluminum hulls among the present boats.

What material would you prefer for the hull of your next boat?

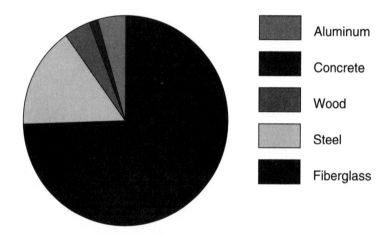

For their next boats, they picked: fiberglass, 75%; steel, 16%; aluminum, 4%; wood, 4%; and ferrocement, 1%.

More interesting is the degree of satisfaction with their present hull materials—the percentages who would choose the same material again: fiberglass, 86%; steel, 57%; and wood, only 16%.

Fiberglass had great appeal both for its low maintenance and its repairability. Steel appealed to a significant number for its safety in case of collision or grounding, although 43% of those who currently owned steel indicated they would switch to aluminum for their next boats. Wood was a big loser because of its high maintenance factor.

What is the draft of your current boat (if a centerboard, with the board up)?

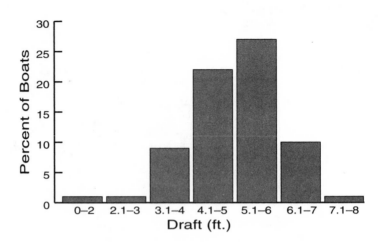

Nearly 70% of all boats had drafts of between 4 and 6 feet. It is noteworthy that not a single person complained of their boat having either too great or too small a draft.

Even more interesting is the lack of correlation between draft and frequency of grounding. Although a deep draft limits where a boat can go, boats with drafts of less than 3 feet grounded as often as boats with drafts over 6 feet. Grounding appears to be mainly a function of diligence.

What is the age of your current boat?

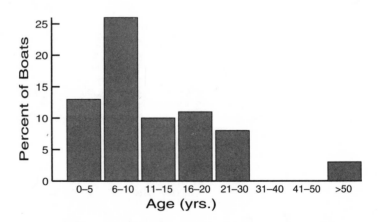

I can think of no reason why so many of the boats were between six and 10 years of age. Why there were three boats over 50 years, but no boats between 30 and 50 years, is likewise a mystery.

Of the three boats over 50 years of age, two were wood and one steel.

2. Rigging & Sails

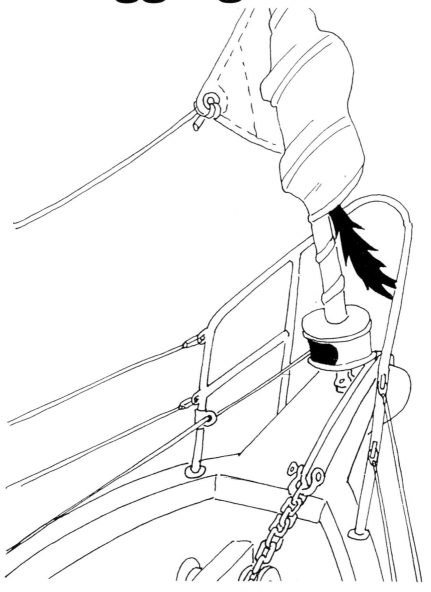

Hon, have you seen the dog since we got in?

Introduction

Rigging and sails are to a sailboat as engine(s) are to a motorboat. Of course, most sailboats also have engines, but they are auxiliary to the main propulsive force of wind against the sails.

Many rigs (arrangement of spars) have evolved over the years. Some rigs stress performance, particularly when going into the wind, while others stress ease of handling. Similarly, specialty sails have evolved for both light and heavy winds.

In addition, there are options for furling the sails, protecting both sailor and sails from the ravages of sunlight, and getting to the top of the mast.

You will find that cruisers favor comfort and safety over speed.

What is the rig of your current boat?

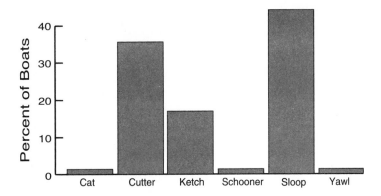

Sloops (44%) and cutters (35%) dominated the current fleet. There were only one each of cat (no jib), schooner (two masts, with foremast equal or smaller than mainmast), and yawl (small mizzenmast aft of steering post).

Ketches (mizzenmast forward of steering post) outnumbered yawls 16% to 1.4%.

What type of rig would you pick next time?

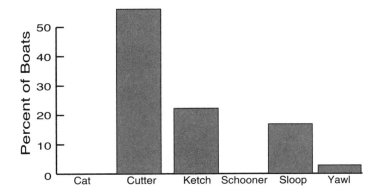

The distribution of rigs the owners would rather have is quite different from that of the current rigs: cutters were desired by 56%, followed by ketches (23%), sloops (18%), and yawls (3%). No one wanted a cat or schooner.

Fifteen sloops defected to cutter rigs and five sloops to ketch rigs. Expressed as degree of satisfaction with their current rigs, they ranked: cutter, 80%; ketch, 78%; and sloop, 26%.

Advantages cited for cutters and ketches over sloops were:
- greater variety of sails
- smaller sails
- shorter mainmast

Do you have a spinnaker (either racing or cruising), and do you use it when appropriate?

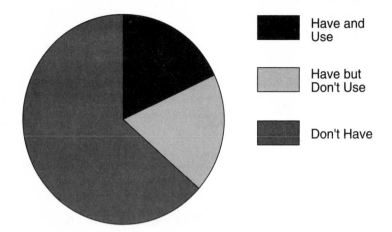

- Have and Use
- Have but Don't Use
- Don't Have

Cruising liveaboards are not racers! Nearly all have genoa jibs, but 64% have neither racing nor cruising spinnakers. Of the 36% who do have spinnakers, half have never used them!

The reasons given fell into two categories:

1. "A spinnaker is too much work."
2. "We're not in a hurry."

Do you carry storm sails, and if so, have you ever used them?

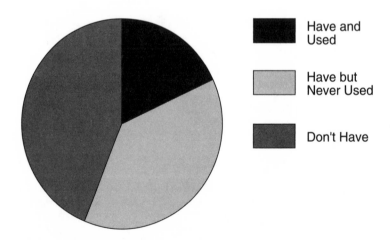

- Have and Used
- Have but Never Used
- Don't Have

More cruisers have storm sails (56%) than spinnakers (36%), but only 18% have had occasion to use them. Many commented that storm sails were, like fisherman anchors, a form of insurance—if you have them, you probably will never need them. Considering the cost of these tiny sails (about $200), it is probably foolish not to carry them.

Do you have, or
would you like to
have, a roller furl-
ing jib?

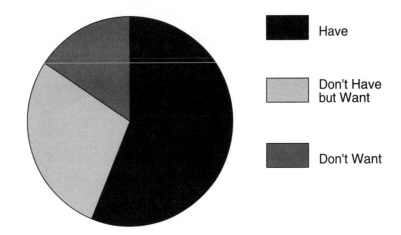

A hefty 85% of the cruisers either have or plan to add a
roller furling jib as soon as finances permit.

Most of those not wanting roller furling jibs cited reliability
and ultimate safety in a storm as reasons for rejection.

Many having roller furling say they now sail a greater percentage of the time due to the ease of sail handling. Even
those favoring roller furlers admit, however, that it is
extremely difficult to furl the sail in winds over 30 knots.

Do you have, or
would you like to
have, a roller furl-
ing mainsail?

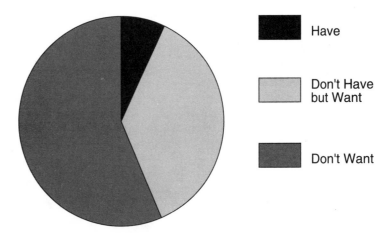

Cruisers are more wary of roller furling mainsails than
jibs. Fifty-six percent wouldn't take one if it were offered
free. Concerns included organ-pipe sounds from the wind
across the mast slot, weakening of the mast, and jam-
ming inside the mast.

That only 7% of the 44% who favor roller furling mains
already have them is due to the high cost of conversion—
about $5,000 to $10,000.

At what apparent (relative to boat) windspeed do you first reef your main-sail?

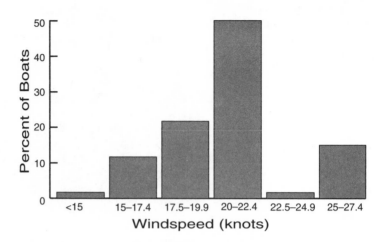

Most cruisers have mastered the art of reefing; 87% report doing so regularly.

They are also conservative. The greatest percentage (50%) take their first reef at apparent windspeeds of between 20 and 22.4 knots to windward, meaning they first reef at true windspeeds of only 15 to 18 knots.

It is interesting that only 2% report reefing at 22.5 to 24.9 knots, while 15% report reefing at over 25 knots. Examining the data, it was found that all of the latter were sailing heavy, stiff displacement boats.

Do you have, or would you like to have, a dodger or pilothouse?

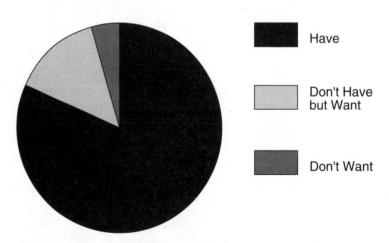

Living on a boat 365 days a year, it doesn't take long before one experiences a truly miserable passage with temperatures in the forties, windchill in the teens, and water dripping down the back of one's neck. Small wonder that 96% of cruisers either have or want a spray dodger or pilothouse.

Do you have, or would you like to have, a bimini (awning over the cockpit)?

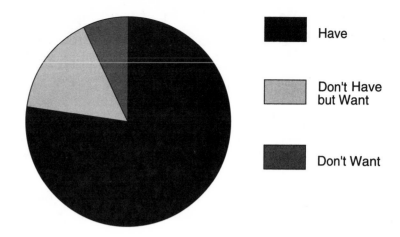

The cruisers in the survey either stayed in southern waters year-round or ventured north only in summer. As a result, they were concerned with excessive sun nearly as much as with cold and rain. Only 7% neither had nor wanted biminis.

Many of the biminis were of the full-enclosure type, zipping up fully against wind and rain, as well as sun. Full-enclosure biminis are the equivalent of sunrooms, increasing the living space and liveability of a small boat dramatically.

You get in late in the day and you're not sure whether you'll be sailing the next day. Would you cover your sails?

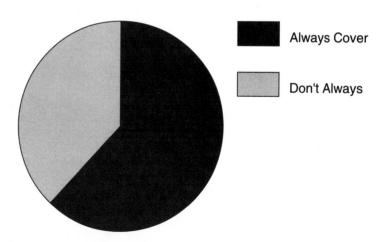

Sixty-two percent claim they *always* cover their sails, regardless of sun conditions or uncertainty of the next day's plans, and about 30% of the rest *nearly always* covered their sails.

The concern for covering sails stems from the ravages of ultraviolet rays, which become obvious in just a few months in the tropical sun.

Do you have and use a bosun's chair?

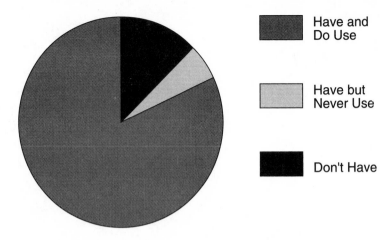

Legend:
- Have and Do Use
- Have but Never Use
- Don't Have

Eighty-seven percent of the boats carried a bosun's chair (canvas chair for hoisting a person to the top of the mast). All but one of the others had steps on the mast. In other words, 99% had a way to get to the masthead.

Although not a survey question, three of the crews knew of people either crippled or killed by falling from the mast. Most crews take mast climbing very seriously, often using safety harnesses and more than one hoisting line.

Do you have mast steps?

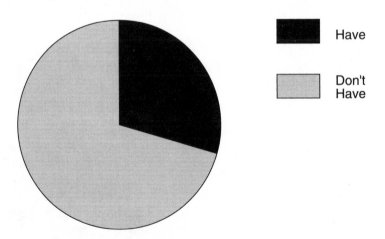

Legend:
- Have
- Don't Have

Thirty percent of the cruisers have installed mast steps. The general feeling is that steps are more secure than a bosun's chair, particularly in a seaway.

When a boat is rolling, the motion at the top of the mast is greatly amplified. A person in a bosun's chair will grip the mast with their thighs (often tightly enough to cause bruising) and the shrouds with both hands, leaving no way to perform the task.

3. Mechanical

Well, I don't see anything wrong. But it doesn't sound very happy.

Introduction

The mechanical and electrical systems on sailboats and motorboats differ more in size than in complexity. Since motorboats are usually either underway with plenty of power from the alternator or plugged in dockside, electrical consumption is not an issue.

Cruising sailboats, on the other hand, are most often anchored or sailing, with electricity being generated only when the auxiliary engine is used to enter or leave an anchorage. Generation, storage, and use of electricity thus become significant problems for the sailor.

Cruising sailors also range farther from "civilization" than their motoring counterparts. Fuel efficiency, range under power, and reliability of mechanical systems are therefore important to the cruiser.

The survey showed that the cruisers wanted more propulsion power, electrical power, electrical storage, fuel storage, and range under power than they currently had. It also uncovered surprising and reassuring statistics regarding the reliability of engines, transmissions, shafts, and propellers.

Finally, considering the performance of the wind and solar systems in the survey, I'm going to invest in alternative energy stocks.

What is the make of your engine?

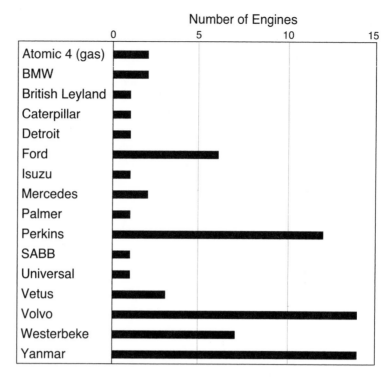

The table above shows the numbers of each engine found. Yanmar, Volvo, Perkins, and Westerbeke are the most popular brands. The Yanmar, a relative newcomer, is found in half of the boats less than seven years old.

Do you consider your engine access adequate?

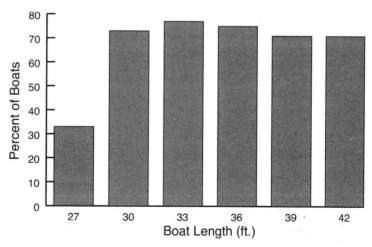

The lack of correlation between engine access and boat size is interesting. Good access does not necessarily require a large engine compartment, but can result from convenient location and a removable engine cover.

In your accumulated years of owning and operating a cruising boat, how many times have you had to repair or replace the following:

One of the biggest bugaboos for the typical novice cruiser is mechanical breakdown. How likely is an engine or transmission failure on a three-month cruise to the Bahamas? How often will I have to repack the stuffing box or replace the cutless bearing? What spare parts should I carry for my engine and other mechanical systems?

First, the cruiser was asked to calculate his engine years—the accumulated years of cruising with typical use of the engine. For example, six years of cruising one month each summer, plus two straight years of cruising would equal (6÷12) + 2 = 2.5 engine years. The engine years for all cruisers totalled 277.

Next, the cruiser was asked how many times he'd had to repair or replace each of 18 mechanical systems or parts.

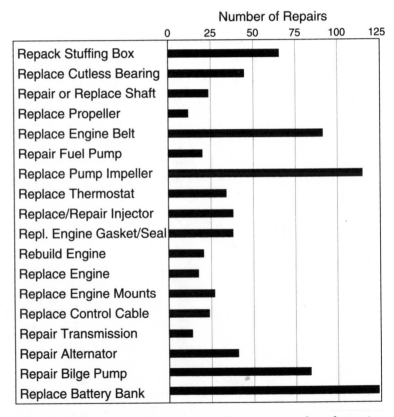

Overall, batteries and pump impellers were replaced most often, while transmissions and propellers gave the fewest problems. In my first two years, I had to replace the propeller once and repair the transmission twice. At the same time, I never replaced either a pump impeller or a battery. Mechanical statistics are no better than life insurance statistics. Both are averages, and neither is a guarantee.

What was the mean time between failures?

By dividing the total engine years by the number of failures, we get what manufacturers call the mean time between failures (MTBF). This is a very useful quantity because it shows us the probability of a particular failure over any time period (with the caveat that the statistics are based on many different brands of equipment and different degrees of owner care and maintenance).

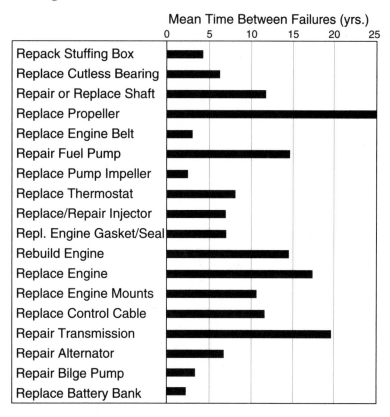

For example, propellers required replacement only 11 times in the 277 engine years. The MTBF is thus 277÷11 = 25.2 years. If we were to install a new or reconditioned propeller just before embarking on a two-year, round-the-world cruise, there is less than a 10% chance that we would have to replace it during the trip.

On the other hand, batteries were replaced 124 times in 277 years, resulting in a MTBF of 2.2 years. The chances of having to replace the batteries during our circumnavigation are about 50/50.

Based on the MTBFs above, I carry the following spares: packing material, engine belts, pump impellers, thermostat, fuel injector, engine gaskets, alternator, and bilge pump kit. I also take *extremely good care of my batteries.*

What was the mean time between rebuilding or replacing engines?

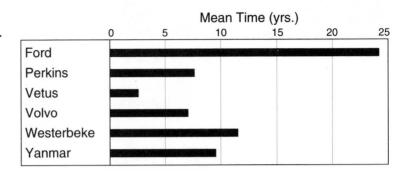

Which is the toughest diesel engine? You should probably ignore the statistics for Vetus (only three engines in survey) and Ford (four engines), but the remaining statistics indicate that the Westerbeke may have a slight advantage over the other brands in terms of longevity.

The often quoted opinion of old-time diesel mechanics that the Japanese Yanmar is too lightweight and too high speed is disputed by these statistics, although it must be noted that the average age of the Yanmars in the survey was only two years.

What was the mean time between all engine repairs?

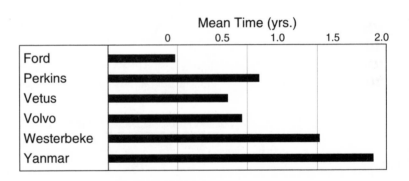

Rebuilding or replacing an engine is expensive, but all repair and maintenance is annoying. The graph above tabulates the MTBF for all engine problems, including: fuel pump, cooling pump impeller, thermostat, fuel injectors, engine gaskets, engine seals, rebuilding, and replacement.

Excluding Vetus and Ford for insufficient data, among the most popular engines in this survey, the Volvo was the most troublesome and the Yanmar the least troublesome.

What is the continuous-rated horsepower of your engine?

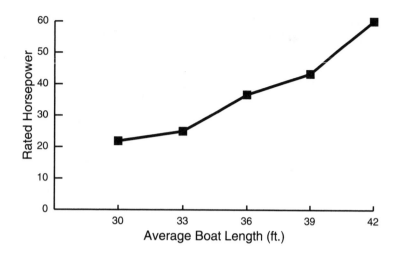

The graph above shows the average continuous-rated (usually nominal) horsepowers for boats of different lengths. In general, most owners felt their boats were slightly underpowered, as shown below.

What do you consider the ideal horsepower for your current boat?

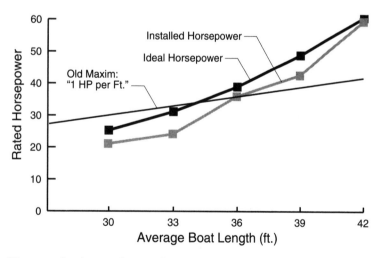

The graph above shows the average horsepower owners feel would be ideal for their boats. The lighter-weight curve is the installed horsepowers from the previous graph. The sloped straight line represents the old rule of thumb "one horsepower per foot of length," a rule that owners obviously feel deficient for boats over 34 feet in length.

What is your boat's installed fuel capacity?

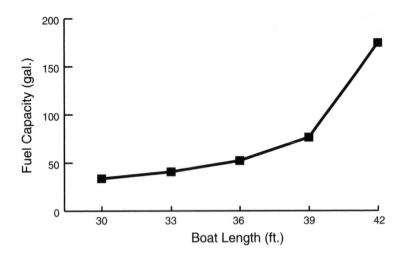

Fuel tanks are often found in similar locations —in the curved space of the bilge for example. The volumes of such spaces are proportional to the cube of the boat's length. Since a 42-foot boat is 1.4 times the length of a 30-foot boat, its fuel tank could be 1.4 X 1.4 X 1.4 = 2.74 times as large, if installed in the same location.

What fuel capacity would you like in your boat?

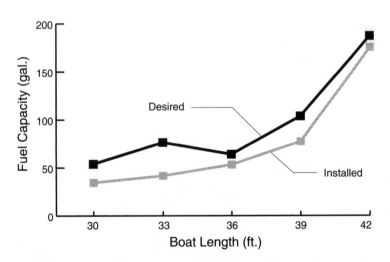

In boats up to 35 feet, the owners usually desired fuel capacities about 50% larger than originally installed. Many carried extra fuel on deck, the amounts averaging 14 gallons for those who carried any at all.

The owners of boats over 40 feet were generally satisfied with their installed capacities.

How many nautical miles per gallon do you average under power alone?

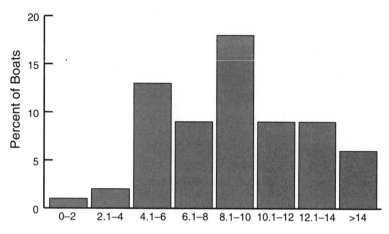

One of the reasons cruisers opt for sail over power is the greater fuel efficiency of sailboat hulls. The graph above shows that the boats surveyed achieved an overall average fuel efficiency of 9.4 nautical miles per gallon (10.9 statute miles per gallon), comparable to that of many luxury automobiles!

estimated fuel efficiency versus length

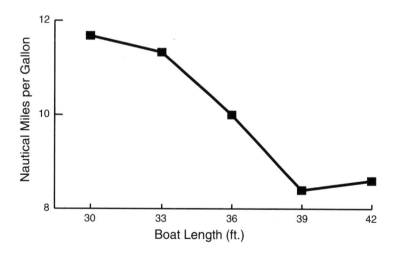

Grouping boats by length ("33" representing lengths 32 to 34 feet for example), demonstrates the higher fuel efficiencies of smaller boats. The efficiencies of the larger boats are still five to 10 times those of similar-size motorboats, however.

What was the estimated range under power alone?

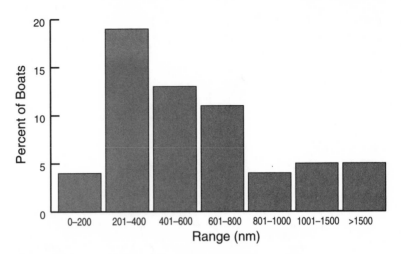

Multiplying installed fuel capacity by fuel efficiency gives the estimated range of the boat under power alone. Most of the smaller boats do not have the 800- to 1,000-nautical-mile range often recommended for extended passagemaking. This is why many small boats carry extra fuel on deck in jerricans.

The average extra fuel carried (14 gallons) times average fuel efficiency (11 nautical miles per gallon) adds an average of about 150 nautical miles to powered range.

estimated range under power versus length

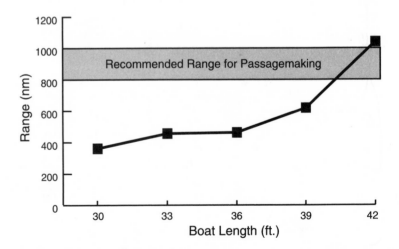

Grouping and averaging by length, shows that boats 40 feet and over tend to have adequate installed fuel capacity for extended passagemaking.

4. Electrical

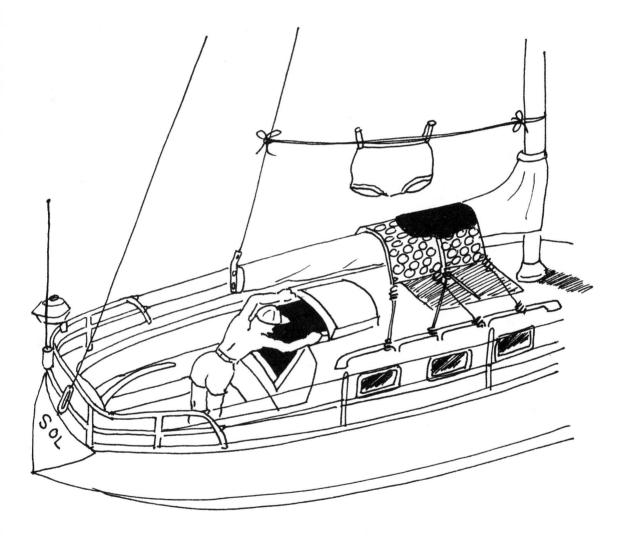

Damn it, Mary Jane, you're shading the collectors again!

Introduction   Other than the integrity of the hull, electricity is probably the most important aspect of a boat. Without it,
most cruisers would be without navigation, communication, refrigeration, lighting, entertainment, and the ability to start their engines.

Most of those surveyed displayed a reasonable facility
with wiring. They were able to isolate and repair broken
wires, corroded connections and blown fuses and lamps.

All comprehension ceased, however, when it came to batteries. Although the battery is the heart and soul of a
boat's electrical system, to the average cruiser what went
on inside the battery box was pure alchemy and a bit of
nasty business to boot.

I have found that maintaining marine batteries is analo-
gous to maintaining house plants. With understanding
and constant attention, they flourish; without, they soon
wither and die. A few of the cruisers had battery green
thumbs. Their Surrettes were in their teens and still
going strong. The rest had either switched to more
expensive, but relatively maintenance-free, gel-cells, or
were in the habit of buying a set of inexpensive Sears
Die-Hards every year.

What is the total capacity of your batteries in amp hours?

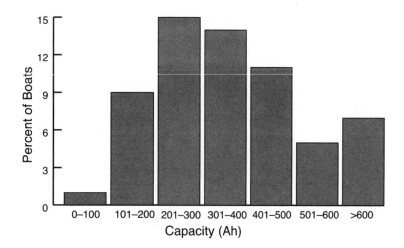

I asked the cruisers for the total amp-hour rating (20-hour discharge rate) of all their batteries, including a separate engine-starting battery if they had one. The overall average was 408 Ah, although the most common size was around 300 Ah.

What battery capacity would you like to have in this boat?

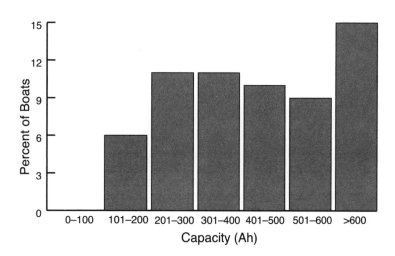

Considering the importance of electricity, it is not surprising that increased battery capacity was one of the cruisers' greatest desires, averaging 518 Ah.

The best deep-cycle marine batteries weigh about 0.8 pound per Ah. Lack of space, not money, is the primary reason most do not add more capacity.

While at anchor for an extended period, how many hours per day do you run your engine to charge your batteries?

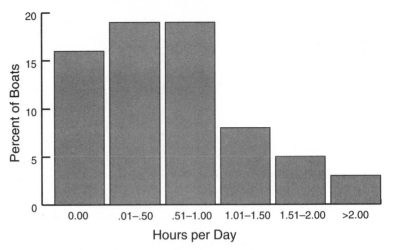

Unless one has alternate energy sources, the engine must be run to recharge the batteries while at anchor. This produces noise, consumes fuel, and wears the engine. Worse, the engine is run under the worst of all conditions—at low rpm and at less than 10% of its rated load.

Do you have a high-output alternator (over 35 amps), an alternator controller, or both?

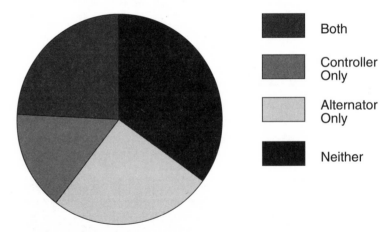

The standard alternator for most diesels is rated at about 35 amps. Half of the boats had installed larger alternators.

Standard, fixed-voltage regulators limit alternator voltage to between 13.8 and 14.2 volts. The result is that alternator current drops as battery voltage rises, so that battery charging takes a long time. Alternator controllers bypass the regulator and can force the alternator to put out maximum current until the battery rises to a cutoff voltage. Though many didn't regularly use them, 39% had installed such devices.

In an effort to speed charging, 24% had installed both larger alternators and alternator controllers.

hours per day of battery charging versus power source

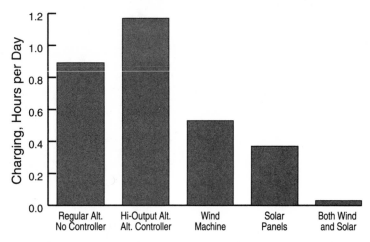

Many things can be done to reduce charging time while at anchor. The first step, which most cruisers seem to have ignored, is to reduce the consumption of electricity by retrofitting with fluorescent and halogen spotlighting and increasing refrigerator insulation.

Much is made in boating articles and advertisements of heavy-duty alternators and alternator controllers, and many cruisers have installed them (see previous page). For whatever reason, however, the devices don't seem to have reduced charging times. Perhaps their installation negates the conservation ethic and encourages consumption.

What clearly do work are the alternative energy sources of wind and sun.

Do you have a wind generator, solar cells, or both?

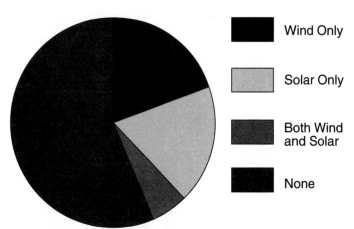

Attempting to reduce the amount of time the engine is run, 23% have installed wind generators, 22% solar panels, and 6% both devices. Both the previous and following graphs demonstrate the effectiveness of these systems.

What percentage of your total power do you estimate you obtain from alternative energy sources?

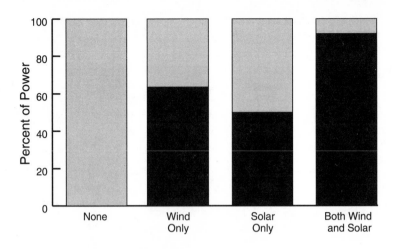

Those with wind generators estimated they derived an average of 60% of their electricity from the wind. Those with solar panels estimated a 42% contribution. Those with *both* wind and solar figured they derived 92% from the combined sources.

If you have a generator, how many hours per week do you run it while at anchor?

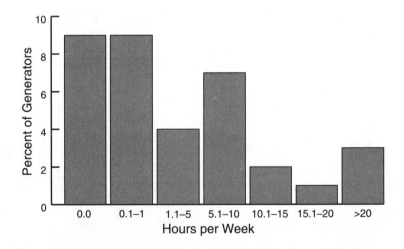

About half (49%) possess auxiliary AC generators. The primary use is not battery charging, however. Uses cited were emergency power for starting the main engine and 110-volt AC power to run tools and appliances such as stoves, microwaves, and televisions. Of course, many have installed DC to AC inverters for the same purpose.

Those who had generators used them an average of 5.8 hours per week, or 0.8 hour per day.

5. Electronics

Dudley tunes up his ham rig.

Introduction

There is no question that boating has entered the electronic age. Most of the surveyed cruisers depended on electronics for communication and navigation. A few had every conceivable electronic device, installed in a navigation station resembling the control console of the space shuttle.

At the opposite extreme, a few diehards communicated a visceral disdain for electronics, and bemoaned the demise of the good old days of pencil and chart piloting, celestial navigation, and sounding by leadline.

The majority, however, had whatever electronics their limited cruising budgets could afford.

What electronic devices do you have aboard your current boat?

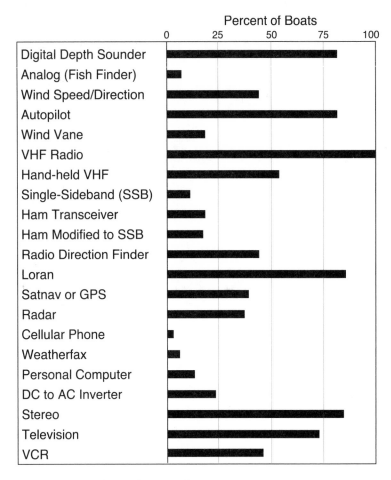

Percent of Boats

Digital Depth Sounder	
Analog (Fish Finder)	
Wind Speed/Direction	
Autopilot	
Wind Vane	
VHF Radio	
Hand-held VHF	
Single-Sideband (SSB)	
Ham Transceiver	
Ham Modified to SSB	
Radio Direction Finder	
Loran	
Satnav or GPS	
Radar	
Cellular Phone	
Weatherfax	
Personal Computer	
DC to AC Inverter	
Stereo	
Television	
VCR	

depth sounders

Three types of depth sounder are:

- Digital—depth indicated by digits.
- Analog—depth indicated by the position of a blinking light on a rotating dial.
- Fish Finder—bottom contour plus intervening reflectors shown on a continuous strip.

Very often a *digital* display will jump from the true depth to a much smaller number (from 50 to 4 feet, for example). This is hard on those with weak hearts. The false signal may be due to air bubbles from a passing wake, a school of fish, or a stronger return signal from the surface than from the bottom. Under the same conditions, an *analog* display will show blips at both 4 and 50 feet, indicating that the 4-foot depth was spurious. A *fish finder* goes a step further, graphically recording the gradual change in depth over the past few minutes, as well as the sudden appearance of the second reflection.

Eighty-two percent of the cruisers had digital depth displayed in the cockpit, while 7% had the older analog display. Most of those with analog instruments said they would not trade for a digital display because of the false reading phenomenon and because the analog display was more immediately understandable.

I found the complete absence of fish finders extremely interesting. I would love to have a fish finder at the helm. My unsubstantiated theory is that sailors associate fish finders with sport fishermen, a species they equate with bottom growth.

wind speed and direction indicators

The tell-tale has gone electronic as well. Electronic wind instruments typically display digital windspeed and analog (with a rotating pointer) wind direction.

In terms of weather conditions, both indications are wrong because they are both relative to the speed and heading of the boat. Some of the newer, more expensive computerized instruments display both true and apparent wind speed and direction. For sailing, however, apparent speed and direction are the criteria by which sails are set.

Forty-four percent had electronic wind instruments. Most of the remaining 56% relied on the heel of the boat and sea state for wind speed and a mast-top wind vane ("Windex") for direction.

The single advantage of the electronic instruments is the ability to monitor relative wind direction or angle of attack from under a dodger or canopy, without developing blindness or a crick in the neck from looking up at the top of the mast.

automatic steering

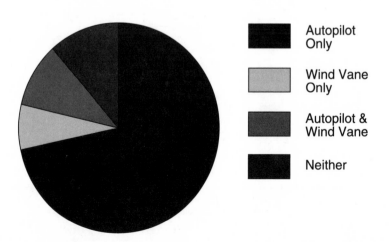

Autopilot Only

Wind Vane Only

Autopilot & Wind Vane

Neither

The thrill of steering wears off quickly when cruising full time. All but 11% of the boats had either an autopilot, a wind vane, or both. Both steering devices relieve the crew of "the tyranny of the wheel."

The cruisers agreed unanimously that either device is the equivalent of adding a crewmember who:

- never complains or tires
- doesn't smell, smoke, eat, or drink
- is superhumanly precise
- is incredibly stupid

As an illustration of the latter characteristic, one sailor told of the first trial of his autopilot. After convincing himself of its infallibility, he entered the precise coordinates of his next waypoint, a navigation buoy, and headed below to mix a congratulatory martini. As he was pouring the drink, the boat shuddered with a fiberglass-rending crunch. The autopilot had followed his instructions exactly and taken him dead-on into the huge steel can.

Autopilots, installed on 82% of the boats, were first developed for motorboats. They hold a boat on a constant magnetic course, either entered on a keypad or dialed in. Both tiller and wheel versions are available. The advantages of the autopilot are:

- ability to hold a precise magnetic course
- adaptability to any size boat
- option for interfacing with Loran and GPS, allowing automatic correction for current and wind set and sequencing of waypoints

Disadvantages of the autopilot include:

- lower reliability
- moderate power consumption

If you have an electronic autopilot, aside from anchoring and docking, what percentage of the time do you use it underway?

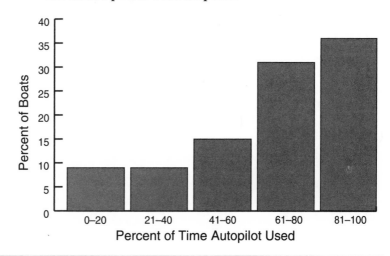

Wind vanes hold a constant heading relative to the wind. Advantages of the wind vane include:

- zero power consumption
- simplicity and high reliability
- maintains constant angle of wind on sail

Disadvantages of the wind vane include:

- failure to work in calm conditions
- failure to hold a constant compass course

If you have a mechanical wind vane, aside from anchoring and docking, what percentage of the time do you use it underway?

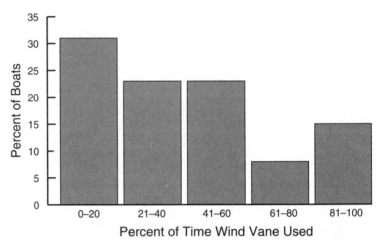

The fact that electrical autopilots are used more often than mechanical wind vanes is a function of neither reliability nor effectiveness. Autopilots are used near shore where precise course is important. Wind vanes are used offshore where angle of wind on sail is more important than course.

How many VHF radios do you have on board (including hand-held)?

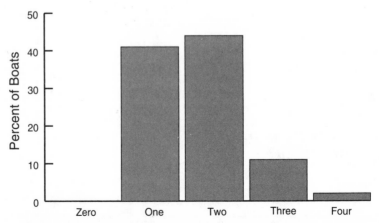

A VHF radio is the most important piece of safety equipment. A second hand-held unit can be used in the cockpit, in a liferaft, or by crew ashore back to the boat.

In transmitting over open water to another boat with the same mast height as your own, what range do you reliably achieve?

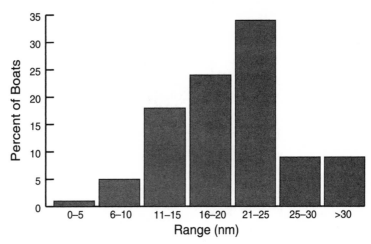

Considering the propensity of sailors to brag, I was surprised at the modest claims made for VHF range.

VHF transmissions are theoretically line-of-sight. The distance in nautical miles from masthead to horizon is $1.17 \times \sqrt{H}$, where H is mast height in feet. Due to some curvature, a common rule is to use 1.4 rather than 1.17. From masthead to masthead the factor becomes 2.8.

With an average surveyed mast height of about 55 feet, the theoretical range is 20.8 nm—almost exactly the same as the average of 21.1 nm claimed.

Do you have an official SSB radio, a ham radio, or a ham radio modified to transmit on SSB channels?

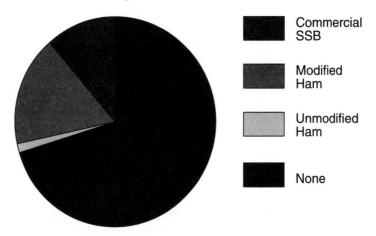

The only way to communicate beyond the 20 to 25 nm range of VHF radio is by High Frequency (HF) radio. These are commonly either Marine Single Sideband radios ("SSBs"), or Amateur (ham) radios. Both function as general coverage receivers from 300 kHz to 30 MHz, receiving worldwide news, high-seas weather, WWV time ticks, high-seas AT&T operators, and weatherfax.

SSBs are restricted to transmitting only on officially designated SSB channels. Ham radios transmit only in official ham bands.

Manufacturers claim the significantly more expensive SSBs are more frequency stable and more reliable in the marine environment. Except for a single, easily-removed diode in the ham version, SSBs and ham units from the same manufacturer often appear to have identical circuitry. That is, by clipping the lead of a single component, one can transmit on SSB channels with a ham radio.

Very few of the cruisers surveyed possessed a ham license, but 18% had installed a ham radio, of which 92% had been modified (diode removed) to transmit on all frequencies, including SSB channels.

It should be pointed out that, strictly speaking, it is illegal to transmit in the ham frequency bands without a ham license, and illegal to transmit on SSB channels without both a SSB license and a certified SSB radio.

Don't imagine that you can simply purchase a ham radio and then start chatting with hams all over the world. Obtaining the level of ham license required for "voice privileges" (the general license) is not easy, and hams who have worked hard to obtain their tickets are not receptive to freeloaders.

It is also illegal to transmit on SSB channels on other than a certified SSB radio (except in case of an emergency, when anything goes). In spite of the legalities, cruisers with modified ham rigs will be heard chatting merrily away all over the East Coast and Caribbean.

Appendix D (pages 138–141) lists the most interesting and useful listening frequencies mentioned by the cruisers.

electronic navigation

The electronic navigation equipment surveyed included radio direction finders, Loran, satnav, GPS, and radar.

Although 44% of the boats had RDFs, most were antiquated and rarely used.

Eighty-six percent had Loran and used it nearly all the time they were underway.

Thirty-nine percent had either satnav (one fix every 90 minutes) or GPS (one fix every second). Nearly every cruiser said they intended to purchase a GPS as soon as the price dropped below $1,000.

Overall, 39% had radar. Significantly, however, 80% of those were from northern areas where fog is common.

My impression was that the cruisers felt the ideal nav station would have radar, GPS, and Loran as a backup to GPS. Very few were interested in electronic charts (at least the ones they'd seen so far) as replacements for the real thing. They were bothered by the lack of detail and lack of color, but most of all by the inability to see both detail and overview at the same time.

entertainment equipment

Eighty-five percent had stereo players, mostly in the form of the ubiquitous automotive AM/FM cassette unit.

An almost equal number (73%) had small TVs. The mix between color and black and white was equal, the most common reason for black and white being lower power consumption.

A rapidly gaining 46% had VCRs as well. Most of the boats with VCRs carried dozens of tapes, which were actively exchanged. Three reasons for the popularity of VCRs are:

- high cost of attending big-screen movies
- lack of transportation to movie theaters
- lack of television programming outside the U.S.

6. The Dinghy

Mary Ann pulls the 6 A.M. duty

Introduction

The dinghy is the cruisers' automobile and pickup truck combined. It takes them to shore and to picnics, it carries their groceries and guests, and it occasionally rescues them from difficult anchoring situations.

As with an automobile, the relationship is often one of both love and hate. When the sky is blue, the waves are small, and the outboard is running, the cruiser is as happy as Water Rat in *The Wind in the Willows.* When the weather is foul and coming aboard with every wave, or when the engine won't run, however, the crew's mood turns foul and happier days are forgotten. Then it is decided that the inflatable will be traded for a fiberglass dink (or vice versa) and that the outboard is a lemon and would better serve as an anchor.

Finding the perfect dinghy and motor is not as simple as buying the best and most expensive models one can find. The cruising lifestyle takes one into picturesque areas where the cost of living may be low, and dinghies and motors are easy targets for theft. The ideal dinghy is tight as a drum but covered with a dozen patches (most of which are merely decorative camouflage). Similarly, the ideal outboard purrs like a kitten but looks like it's been run over by a tank.

After using their dinghies nearly every day for an average of over two years, the cruisers in the survey had formed definite opinions regarding the characteristics one should look for.

Of what material is your (primary) dinghy constructed?

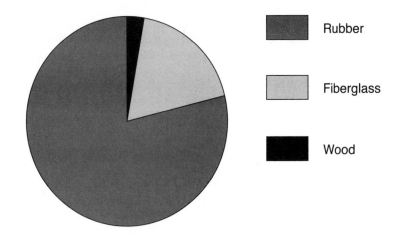

Dinghies fall into two categories: inflatable (rubber) and rigid (fiberglass and wood). The characteristics of the two are diametrically opposed. Inflatables are unsinkable, wouldn't capsize if Godzilla stepped on the gunnel, carry incredible loads, and are easily stowed on deck. On the other hand, they row like a plastic wading pool, require large outboards, are wet into the wind, and cost twice what you would expect.

Rigid dinghies row like a charm, require little power, and can be found used for little money. But they'll flip over if you look at them cross-eyed, and they go bump in the night against the hull.

Of what material do you think your next dinghy will be constructed?

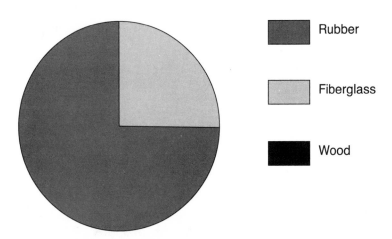

With the exception of wood, the cruisers were fairly satisfied with their present dinghies, although they all represented compromise. The two wood dinks were scuttled and three inflatables defected to fiberglass. Overall, however, 75% still favored the inflatable.

What is the Coast Guard rated capacity of your dinghy in persons?

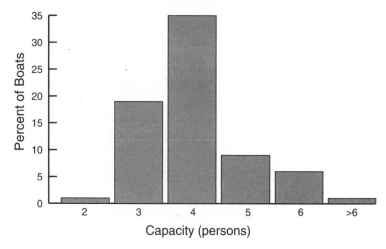

The four-person dinghy (8- to 9-foot inflatable) was judged ideal for a crew of two. It will carry the normal crew plus groceries, or it will carry two couples on an excursion. The three-person dinghy (6- to 7-foot inflatable) is similarly ideal for a singlehander. Most of the five- and six-person dinghies were found on boats with families.

If you were to undertake a 40-nm offshore passage, would you ordinarily tow your dinghy or bring it aboard?

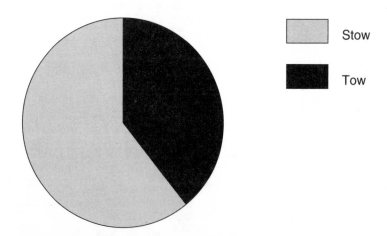

Towed dinghies can be lost, bump into the stern in a following sea, capsize in rough seas, and foul the prop when the tow rope is left too long.

Most cruisers evolve a simple system for hoisting the dinghy aboard after just a few months. Some install davits, but most hoist it over the lifelines with a halyard, swing it aboard, and tie it down amidships or on the foredeck.

Sixty-one percent said they bring the dinghy aboard whenever they venture into open ocean. A significant number bring it aboard even in the calm waters of the ICW.

Have you ever had a dinghy stolen?

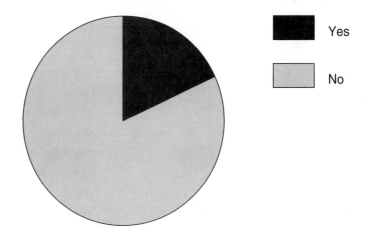

Eighteen percent reported dinghies stolen—some more than once. Dividing by the average number of years aboard, 3.89, it appears that your dinghy stands about a 5% chance of being stolen per year.

You can improve your odds by exercizing extreme care in Nassau (where half of all the thefts occurred), by installing a dinghy lock (see graph below), and by camouflage. Camouflaging a dinghy consists of spilling paint on it, having mismatched and unvarnished oars, and plastering a dozen patches randomly on the tubes.

Do you lock your dinghy when you take it ashore?

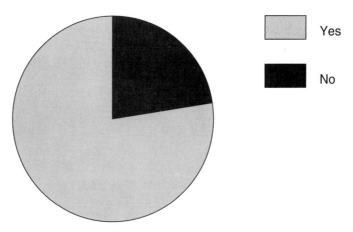

Seventy-eight percent lock their dinghies at the dock, including all but one of those who had experienced theft.

A proper lock consists of stainless aircraft cable Nico-pressed to an eyebolt through the transom and locked to itself with a hefty brass and stainless combination lock. Not even the best system will foil the dedicated thief with a hydraulic bolt cutter, but among a dozen less protected dinghies at a dock, yours will be last to go.

What is the brand of your dinghy outboard?

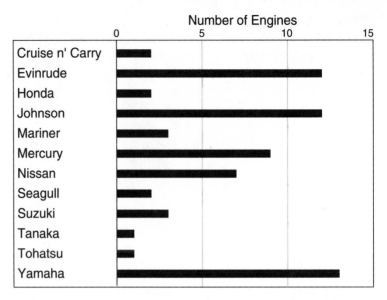

Yamaha outboards enjoyed the best reputation, followed by Johnson and Evinrude. Getting parts for Japanese outboards is no more difficult than for Japanese autos.

Exposed to salt spray continually, outboards are more troublesome than diesels. A majority of the cruisers were adept at disassembling at least their outboard's carburetor, and 25% carried small backup "weedwackers"—the little air-cooled Cruise 'n Carries and Tanakas.

What is the horsepower of your dinghy outboard?

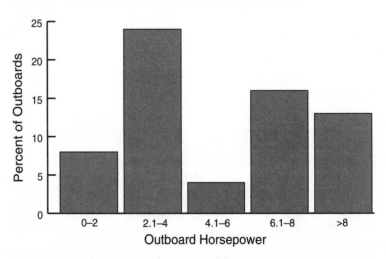

Two sizes of outboard are most popular. Four hp is sufficient to propel any dinghy at less than planing speeds. In fact four hp will plane most four-person inflatables with only one passenger. Eight hp will bring most inflatables to a plane even when fully loaded.

What horsepower do you consider ideal for your current dinghy?

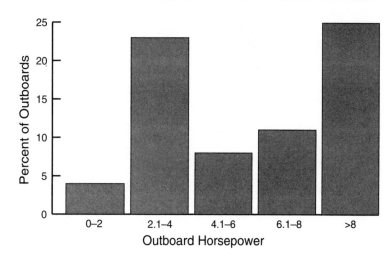

Of the twelve sailors with outboards up to 2 hp, eight were dissatisfied and wanted more power. The 4-hp engine retained its 24% popularity. The biggest increase was in the over 8-hp categories, which jumped from 14% to 25%.

On the basis of what the cruisers wished they had, we can say there are two ideals:

- 4 hp for those who don't care to plane
- 8 to 10 hp for those who do want to plane

It should be remembered that these statistics are for primary outboards. Many sailors carried an extra 1- to 2-hp outboard as a backup.

ideal horsepower versus dinghy size

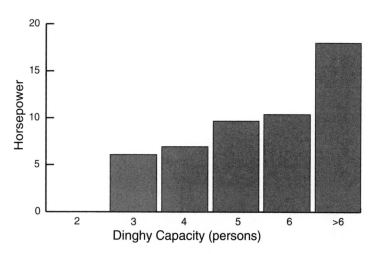

For larger dinghies a useful statistic is the average horsepower desired for each size, as shown above: three-person, 6.1 hp; four-person, 6.9 hp; five-person, 9.7 hp; six-person, 10.4 hp; over six-person, 18 hp.

Have you ever had an outboard stolen?

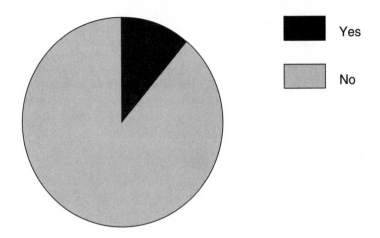

Although 18% reported stolen dinghies, only 11% had lost outboard engines. It appears that dinghies without engines are even more likely to be stolen than those with engines.

Is your outboard locked to your dinghy?

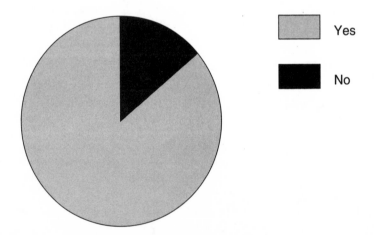

Eighty-six percent locked their outboard engines to their dinghies. Of the eight who had outboards stolen, all now lock the two together.

There are two simple ways to lock an engine to a dinghy:

    1. Padlock the mounting screw handles together so that they cannot be loosened.

    2. Pass the dinghy-lock cable through the outboard before attaching to the dock.

7. The Galley

At sea, everyone looks forward to chowtime.

Introduction

The galley is the boat's kitchen. Nothing is more important to a sailor than his stomach, so the galley is most often the heart of the boat.

At some point beyond day and weekend sailing, one suddenly realizes that meals on a boat can be just as good as meals on land. That realization came to me in Georgetown, Bahamas, while listening to a radio conversation between two cruising women.

"Oops, I've got to go. My toast is up," said the first.

Long silence—then, "You have a toaster on board?"

"Sure. It runs off the inverter, just like the microwave."

"I'm going to kill you!"

My sentiments, exactly. But when I returned to the States, I installed a hefty inverter, and then in rapid order: toaster, microwave, blender, mixer, and coffee grinder. I've been enjoying English muffins and fresh-ground coffee ever since.

The things that are more difficult to come by on a boat are the basics of any kitchen: counter space, storage space, plenty of water (both hot and cold), a good stove and oven, and refrigeration. The survey concentrated on these basics.

What is the capacity of your built-in water tanks?

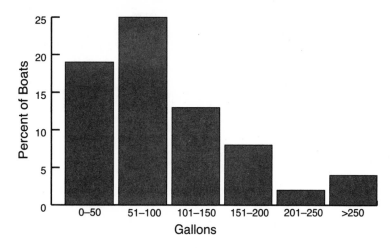

The average American consumes 150 gallons of water per day, including bathing, washing the car, and watering the lawn. Last year my wife and I spent 80 days in the Bahamas and, by practicing extreme conservation, consumed only 90 gallons from our 130-gallon tank. Cruisers have developed water conservation to the point where one half gallon per person, per day is possible, and one gallon per day is extravagance. I've listed some of their water-saving tricks in Appendix C (pages 135–137).

What built-in water capacity would you like to have on your current boat?

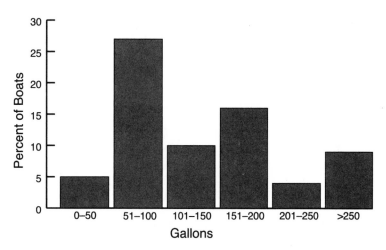

Everyone would like to have unlimited water. To keep the responses realistic, I reminded each sailor that a greater water capacity meant less space for fuel and other storage. The answers thus represent the trade-offs the cruisers would be willing to make in order to have more water.

The graph shows that only 5% found less than 50 gallons acceptable, but that nearly 30% found 50 to 100 gallons OK.

water capacity versus
boat length

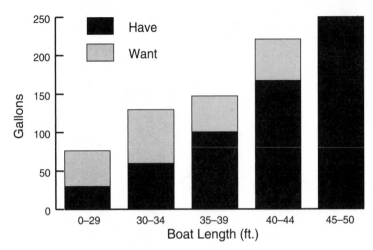

The graph above is even more telling. The solid bars show what water capacity you can expect to find in production boats of different sizes. The total height of the bars shows what liveaboards feel would be more appropriate.

Adding fixed water tanks is extremely difficult and expensive, so use this graph as a guide when you shop for a boat.

Does your galley
have?

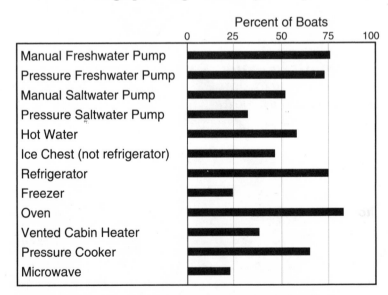

freshwater pumps

Nearly equal numbers of boats have manual or foot-operated freshwater pumps and electrical (pressure) pumps. Many boats have both. But when water becomes scarce, most pull the plug on the pressure pump.

A story one couple told me illustrates the reason why. The couple had invited friends with a child aboard for a week-long cruise. With 150 gallons aboard, they had never before run out of water and so never thought to lecture their guests on water conservation. They left the couple aboard for a few hours in the afternoon while they ran errands. That night the cook was shocked to find the tank empty. Upon questioning, it was found that the little boy was bored, so his mother had allowed him to play with his toy boat in the sink, letting the water run, as he did at home.

It is wondrous how slowly the water disappears when it takes six strokes to fill an 8-ounce cup!

saltwater pumps

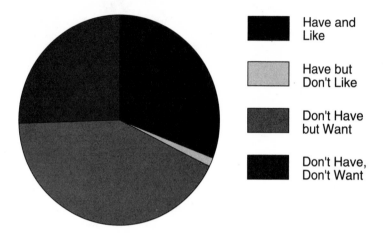

Have and Like

Have but Don't Like

Don't Have but Want

Don't Have, Don't Want

Slightly more than half of the boats had manual salt-water pumps in the galley. Preliminary washing with salt water is one of the most common tricks for saving fresh water, as you'll see in Appendix C.

Thirty-two percent had pressure saltwater pumps as well. Most are connected to a washdown hose that is used to wash mud off the anchor and chain. Some, however, also feed a spigot in the galley. Sixty-three percent of those without a washdown hose wished they had one.

hotwater heaters

Only 21% of the boats under 35 feet had water heaters, but 81% of those over 35 feet did. All but one of the heaters were of the type with both a 110-volt AC element for plugging into dockside power and a heat exchanger for running off the engine. Since most boats ran their engines an hour per day, even at anchor, the larger boats usually had a small supply of hot water every day.

Many of the boats complained of a rotten egg (hydrogen sulfide) smell in their hot water. It is likely that they were heating their water tanks every day, but only drawing off a gallon or two of water, thus encouraging a colony of bacteria in the tank. A shock dose (2 to 3 tablespoons) of chlorine cures the problem.

refrigeration

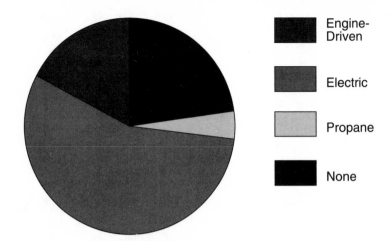

Engine-Driven

Electric

Propane

None

Seventy-five percent of the boats had refrigeration of some kind. Forty-seven percent had an ice box, and 23% had both a refrigerator and an ice box.

Refrigeration was nearly as touchy a subject as finances. I learned to approach the subject gingerly, as many of the 25% without refrigeration responded defiantly. A common response was, "Why would anyone want refrigeration? Once you get used to it, warm beer tastes just as good!" The problem, however, seems to run deeper. One couple renewed what was apparently an ongoing battle in front of me with the woman all but threatening divorce if she didn't get a refrigerator soon.

Adding refrigeration to an existing boat most often requires modification of the ice box, running refrigerant lines through difficult spaces, finding a well-ventilated and dry space for the condenser, doubling the electrical drain on the batteries, laying out from $600 to $2,000, and comprehending a subject few have the background or patience to master.

In spite of the difficulties of installation, most of those with existing systems were happy with their performance. Seventy-two percent of the systems were 12-volt DC, 22% were engine-driven, and 6% ran on propane. The degree of satisfaction results surprised me. Only 8% were not perfectly satisfied with their 12-volt systems, but 25% of the engine-driven and 33% of the propane owners were dissatisfied.

I had read much about the superiority of engine-driven systems. They were supposedly capable of greater cooling, were more reliable, and required running only once per day. In fact, they were capable of large cooling loads, but they required a lot of attention (mostly recharging

satisfaction with refrigeration

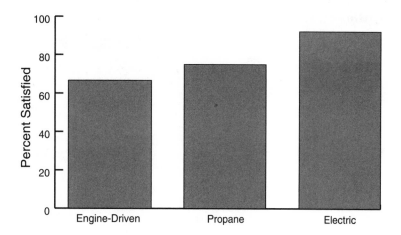

refrigerant, which seems to slowly escape from the flexible hoses). The requirement to run the engine only once a day was true enough, but there was often no other reason to do so, and, with an electric system, this could have been avoided. Their owners also had to find boat sitters to run the engine when they were away.

The few problems with the 12-volt systems were all associated with the evaporator, the little box that holds the ice cube trays. Either the thin aluminum had corroded through or the cook had stabbed one of the capillary tubes with an ice pick. Both actions resulted in total loss of the refrigerant and replacement of the $200 evaporator.

frozen foods

One-third of those with refrigerators carried "significant amounts" of frozen food. This meant either they were running their refrigerators very cold, or they had a separate freezer. It also means that 75% of all the boats had essentially no frozen food, and probably explains why cruisers, as a group, are more vegetarian than average. Two reasons for the sparsity of freezers are higher power consumption and frequency of loss.

The latter is amplified by an amusing vignette that still brings a smile to my face. I encountered a group of boats traveling together in the Bahamas. The largest boat was clearly the leader. Regardless of weather, when she left, they all left.

While interviewing one of the smaller boats, the crew let slip the reason. The big boat had a big freezer, well stocked with pork loin, prime rib, strip steak, even Ben and Jerry's ice cream. Twice, in the past two months, the big freezer had died, and there had been a feeding frenzy in the fleet.

From that point on, whenever I thought of the group, I pictured sea gulls following a fishing boat.

galley stoves

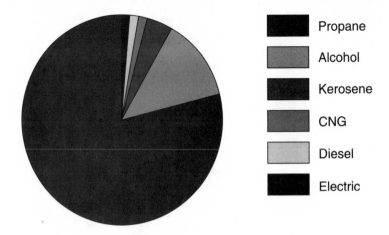

Propane

Alcohol

Kerosene

CNG

Diesel

Electric

The first choice of fuel for galley stoves and ovens was clear: 79% propane. The other fuels were alcohol 12.6%, kerosene 4.6%, and diesel, CNG and electricity each 1.4%.

Propane is available throughout the world (although a variety of adapters should be carried for filling the tanks). Fuel consumption averages about one 14-pound tank per month. Most boats carry two tanks, allowing a month to find a refilling station. Marinas do not generally sell propane, although they always know where to get it. RV travel parks are a common source.

Among alcohol stoves the Origo was the clear favorite. The owners raved about their simplicity (a wad of absorbent batting stuffed into a stainless canister), their heating capacity, and their safety. The stoves held about one quart of fuel and consumed about one gallon of fuel per month.

Kerosene owners were not pleased with any aspect of their stoves and were looking forward to the day they could afford conversion to propane.

The owner of the diesel stove compared it to a woodburning cast iron stove and raved about its performance and its ability to heat the boat in cold weather. Since migrating south, however, he found the heat production intolerable and was using an Origo alcohol stove as backup.

Compressed Natural Gas (CNG) is lighter than air and won't collect in the bilge. It is, therefore, safer than propane. The one CNG owner found it too difficult to procure, however, and planned to convert to propane.

A single boat had an electric range that required a five-kilowatt diesel generator. Not realizing the ramifications, I accepted the owners' generous offer of a cup of coffee. I was mortified, but they apparently saw nothing strange at all about firing up the generator to brew my single cup.

cooking ovens

Overall, 83% had cooking ovens. Boat size is a strong determinant—90% of the boats over 30 feet had ovens, but only 25% of those under 30 feet did.

cabin heaters

Being from Maine, where even the summers can be cold and damp, I was interested in whether cruisers had cabin heaters. After all, their boats were their homes, and how many homes, even in Florida, have no source of heat? Stoves and ovens were not included unless they were vented to the outside because they produce too much water vapor to be used as acceptable heaters. So, disallowing galley stoves, 62% did *not* have cabin heaters. They simply followed the sun and found the few cold spells tolerable. One sailor put it, "This summer has been the longest one I can remember—it's been going on seven years now!"

microwaves and pressure cookers

Even with propane, galleys are so small and the weather so warm that the cooks try to reduce cooking times. Those with plenty of AC power (those with AC generators or large batteries and inverters) usually had small microwaves (22%). Most of the others had pressure cookers (65%). Some had both.

In addition to cooking faster, about 25% of the pressure-cooker owners canned meat and fish along the way.

What percentage of meals do you serve on paper plates?

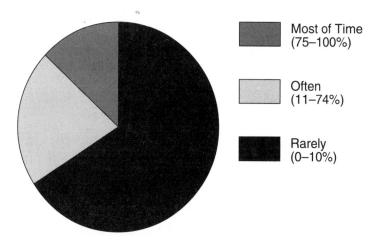

Most of Time (75–100%)

Often (11–74%)

Rarely (0–10%)

Thirty-seven percent scoffed at the paper plate question and claimed they never ever used them. I didn't pursue the matter further, but felt distinct philosophical vibrations.

Sixty-six percent (including the scoffers above) used paper for less than 10% of their meals.

On the other hand, a heretic 13% used paper plates at least 75% of the time. The lesson is to know who you are serving before hauling out the paper china.

Do you ever (such as when fresh water is hard to obtain) wash your dishes in salt water?

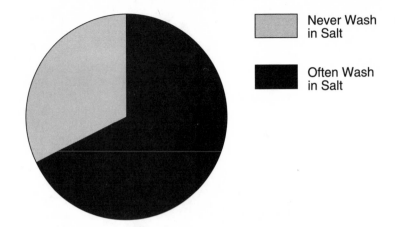

Never Wash in Salt

Often Wash in Salt

Overall, 68% washed dishes in salt water at least some of the time. This may seem a strange notion to someone who sails on Long Island Sound, but it seems less strange when confronted with a 50-gallon water tank and a month to go. When you discover that the ocean water in the Bahamas is cleaner than the drinking water of most major cities, and that most dishwashing detergents don't know the difference between salt and fresh, the salt-water wash seems the only way to go. Drying the dishes immediately and then rinsing the towels in fresh water avoids a salt residue.

The size of the water tank had a strong effect, however. Some of those with 200-gallon tanks weren't aware that washing in salt water was possible. Those who did wash in salt had tanks averaging just 93 gallons and those who didn't averaged 188 gallons.

8. The Head

Ralph carefully weighs his alternatives

Introduction

A great quandary for the liveaboard boater is what to do about head (human) waste. The Environmental Protection Agency (EPA) and most states insist that human waste not be discharged within three miles of shore. They expect boaters to store waste from the head in holding tanks until pumped out at a shore station or pumped overboard at sea. But, in many areas of the U.S., there are no pumpout facilities, so the boater is faced with a dilemma.

I remember being anchored in the Potomac River in Washington, DC. At the foot of Maine Avenue, just a few blocks from EPA Headquarters, there are several hundred liveaboards in slips. One, I hear, is a U.S. Congressman. I asked one of the dockmasters where I could get a holding tank emptied. "Beats me," he said. "I hear there's a place a couple of miles down the river."

The Coast Guard is charged with enforcing the federal head legislation. Their policy appears to be to check for head violations only when a boat is boarded for other reasons. If they then find a violation, you will most likely receive a citation.

Liveaboards have learned to live with both the head and the holding tank dilemma, as you will see in this chapter.

Does your boat have a waste holding tank (whether or not operational)?

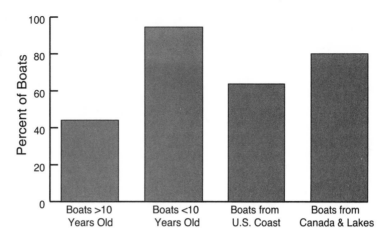

Head laws are strictly enforced in Canadian waters, U.S. lakes, and in some coastal states, but less than half of the boats over ten years old even had a holding tank! Since it has been illegal to sell new boats without holding tanks for about a decade, it is not surprising that 95% of the newer boats had the tanks.

Is your waste holding tank operational (could you quickly demonstrate its operation to a Coast Guard inspector)?

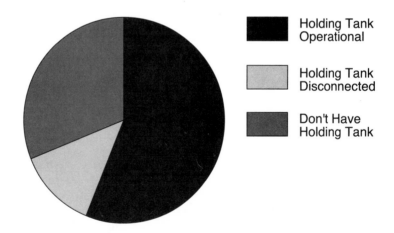

The law does not stipulate how the head waste be stored —only that it not be discharged. Some of those without tanks carried "porta-pottys" for which they had paid less than $100. Most of these had never been used. It was suggested that a token deposit be made lest the Coast Guard suspect they were just a stage prop.

One sailor claimed that when boarded he had stuffed a plastic garbage bag into the bowl as if it were a wastebasket. The Coast Guard inspector gave him a very strange look, but didn't say a word!

Boats with holding tanks most often have a Y-valve that directs the waste either into the holding tank or overboard. When the Coast Guard inspects your head and holding tank within the three-mile limit, they are looking for an indication that waste is not presently being discharged overboard, which would require significant effort and awareness of the captain. It helps to display a prominent note from the captain next to the valve promising death or other appropriate penalty to anyone tampering with the valve within the three-mile limit. Some also either remove the Y-valve handle or wire it in the proper position.

When a guest uses your head, do you worry that it has an objectionable odor?

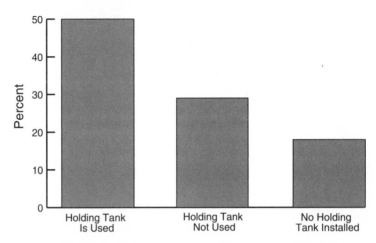

There was a correlation between the use of holding tanks and head odor. Of those having no holding tank, only 18% thought their head smelled bad. Of those who had a tank but didn't use it, 29% reported odor. But among those who used the tank, 50% thought their heads smelled.

Holding tanks aren't the only source of odor, as the 29% who didn't use their tanks but still had odor shows. People who had used thin-walled "bilge-pump hose," instead of the thicker and more expensive "sanitation hose," reported that the smell just seemed to "ooze through the hose."

On average, how many times per year has your head or discharge hose required disassembly to unclog?

A few just couldn't seem to get it right, disassembling the infernal devices on a monthly basis. Most, however, had discovered the golden head rule: "Put nothing in the bowl you haven't eaten." When that rule was obeyed, many heads had required no more than occasional tightening of the packing nuts for as many as five years.

Most excepted reasonable amounts of toilet paper from the golden rule. Others insisted on strict interpretation. I didn't pursue the subject into its farthest creeks, but some volunteered that the used TP went into a zip-lock bag to be thrown out with the rubbish. Others used wash cloths,

times per year head is blocked

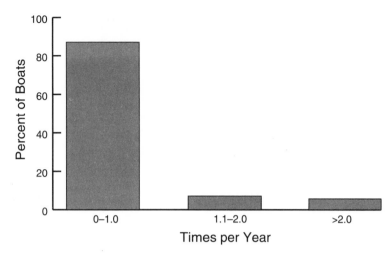

rinsing after every use. "Where *would* you store six-months' supply of toilet paper on a 28-foot boat?" they asked.

One prohibition all agreed upon was Bounty paper towels. A story explains why. Soon after a female guest disembarked, the head plugged up. Upon disassembly it was found that the blockage was farther down the line in the discharge hose. Several hours of probing and reaming with a snake showed the blockage to be at the through hull. Overboard went the plumber (captain), into the through hull went the snake, and out came a Bounty towel—as pristine as the day of its manufacture. Plastic fiber-reinforced Bounty towels are as indestructible as their maker claims.

The survey also uncovered a mysterious head problem and its cure. A sailing doctor explained that the mineral deposit inside the discharge hose (which can totally block a hose

On average, how many times per year does your head need repair (not just clogged)?

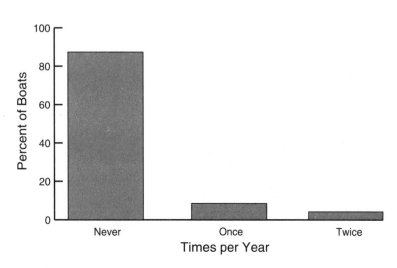

in a year or two) is calcium carbonate, precipitated from the sea water by urine. Many cruisers found that a weekly cup of vinegar flushed down the head and left to reside in the hose overnight will prevent the accumulation.

Separate from the discharge hose, the more complex head and its pumping system proved quite resilient. Only one in 10 required repair as often as once per year. The mean time between repairs was about two years.

9. Anchoring

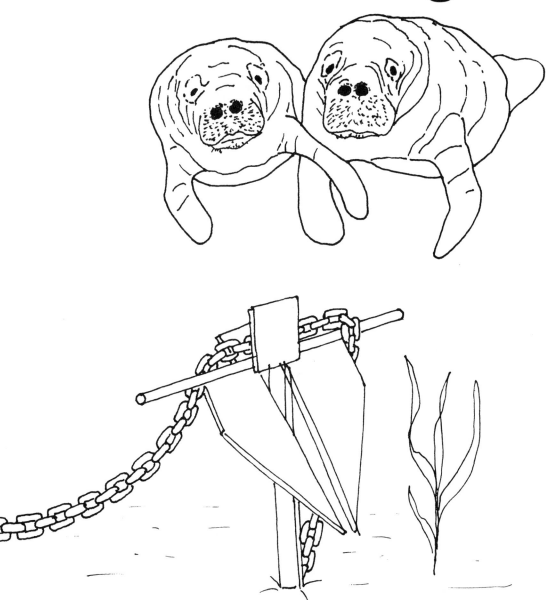

It's a human artifact. Humans are incredibly stupid, but they are multiplying.

Introduction

More than one cruiser advised me, "Cruising is ten percent getting somewhere and then ninety percent trying to stay there."

They are right. If you are the typical liveaboard cruiser, over the course of a year, you will spend an average of one day a week underway and the rest at anchor. That is a lot of anchoring.

Once you cast off from your home port, you are in for a crash course in anchoring. Running the Intracoastal Waterway and cruising the Florida Keys or the Bahamas, you experience anchoring in tides from six inches to 10 feet, bottoms from diaphanous ooze to hard coral, tidal currents from zero to four knots, and anchorages from 50-foot-wide creeks to open waters.

But be assured, you *will* master anchoring. In fact you may come to prefer anchoring over a slip in the most luxurious marina. After many harrowing and ego-damaging experiences, you and your crew will pride yourselves in your anchoring technique.

In this chapter the cruisers share what they have learned about anchoring.

While living aboard, what percentage of nights do you anchor or moor, rather than take a slip?

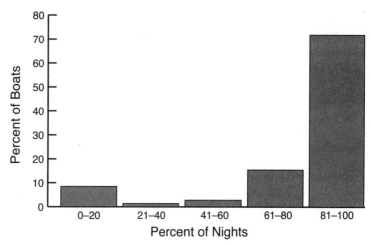

The graph above verifies the statement that you will spend six of seven days "on the hook."

A few lived most of the year in marinas, while they worked to accumulate a cruising kitty. I interviewed them while they were on their annual cruise. Many marinas in Florida cater to this type of liveaboard. For $5 per foot per month, you get a permanent address, a place for your car, a message service, hot showers, laundry room, security guard, and a whole bunch of similar-minded neighbors. On the graph these folks are the 8% anchoring only 0 to 20% of nights.

What is your primary reason for anchoring rather than taking a slip?

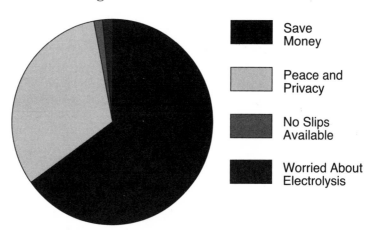

After dragging a few times, there comes a point when you *know* when the hook is down. At that point you begin to prefer anchoring to a slip. When asked their primary reason for anchoring, most balked at having to pick one reason. The statistics don't show it, but at least 80% answered both money and privacy. When forced to choose, 65% settled on money and 32% on peace and privacy.

What do you consider your primary (most often used) anchor?

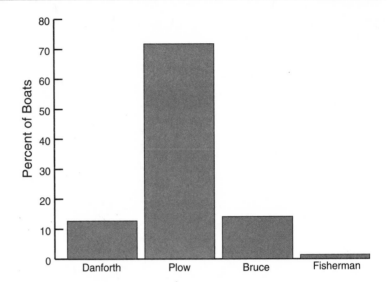

Anchor manufacturers are fond of sponsoring "unbiased tests" of their anchors against those of their competitors. The tests usually consist of measuring the maximum pull exerted by a tow boat before the anchor pulls out or fails. I have no doubt about the veracity of the test results, but I have serious reservations about their relevance to cruising. The maximum load you can put on an anchor is just one of many factors and not usually the one that results in your dragging. How quickly will the anchor set? How quickly will it reset if pulled out? Will it pull out when the direction of pull is reversed? Can it be set at all in strong currents? Will it foul itself if you drop 50 feet of chain on top? Is it fond of picking up lawn chairs and other bottom junk?

I was thus interested in this question: "Never mind what others *say*, never mind what you have *read*, never mind what you *think*—which anchor do you *use* most often?" The results speak loudly: plow, 72%; Bruce, 14%; Danforth, 13%; fisherman, 1%.

plow

The plow is slow to set. Sometimes it requires two tries. Once in, however, it is unlikely to come out. The boat can swing, the wind can shift, the current can reverse, but the plow just turns in its furrow and follows your boat around like a faithful dog.

Bruce

Being one solid piece, the Bruce is easier to handle than either the plow or the Danforth. Its shovel-like fluke digs into mud and sand very quickly, and it follows a swinging boat nearly as well as the plow. The one problem mentioned by several owners was that, when breaking out, it sometimes picks up a clod of clay looking like a cube of earth with a handle. In that condition, it will not reset.

What type is your second anchor?

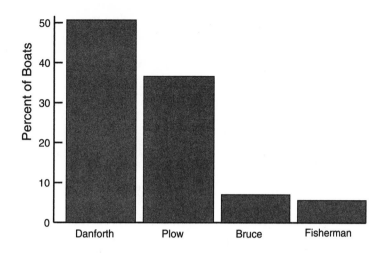

Danforth

The Danforth (type, not brand) has long been a favorite of the weekend sailor. It has tremendous holding power for its weight, it sets very quickly in most conditions, and there are a lot of cheap imitations. For single-anchoring situations, however, it has a fatal flaw. If current or wind reverse, the Danforth will sometimes flip out. Chances are that it will reset; however, when it's the only thing holding your $100,000 boat off the shore, and you are asleep below, are you willing to take the chance? Obviously, only a minority of the cruisers I interviewed were.

fisherman

The fisherman anchor (also know as hurricane insurance) is a terrific anchor that sets easily and holds well in most bottoms. Most don't use it because it is nearly impossible to heft aboard and, unless you have a schooner bowsprit, will bang your topsides in rough going.

What type is your third anchor?

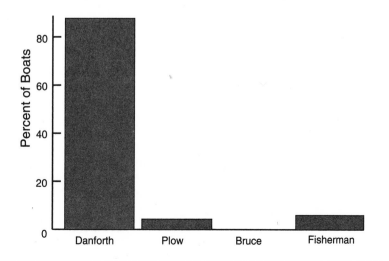

When used as the second anchor in a two-anchor situation, the Danforth has no liabilities. Since the pull is always in the same direction, there is little danger of its flipping out. That explains its popularity as a second anchor.

As a third anchor, used primarily for kedging off (setting an anchor off the stern and winching a grounded boat back in the direction from which it arrived), the Danforth is perfect. Eighty-eight percent of all third anchors were of the Danforth style.

Fortress

There is a new member of the "Danforth family." The Fortress is a high-strength aluminum alloy anchor patterned after the Danforth. Both of its unique characteristics relate to its light weight. On the plus side, a Fortress weighing just 15 pounds has the same holding power as a Danforth weighing 45 pounds. That has great appeal to the 105-pound foredeck mate in charge of the anchor. But hold on—that same lightness can make the Fortress sail like a kite when you're trying to get it down in a strong current. At the very least, it requires a long length of chain to hold it down long enough to dig in.

What is the weight of your primary anchor?

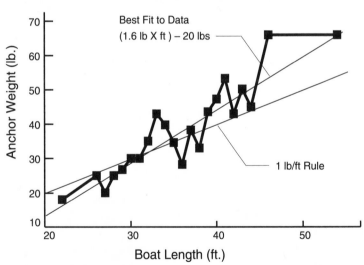

The holding power of steel anchors is proportional to size and, therefore, weight. Weight also contributes to speed when digging in.

I have always heard you should have an anchor (steel only) of weight in pounds equal to the length of your boat in feet. According to the survey, it's not a bad rule, but the formula (1.6 X feet) – 20 pounds fits the data even better. For a 40-foot boat you'd thus want (1.6 X 40) – 20, or 44 pounds.

What is the length of chain on your primary anchor?

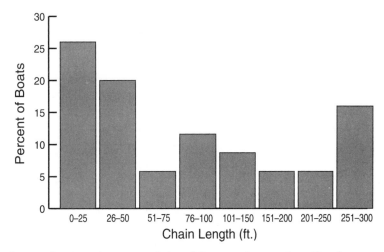

An anchor system consists of the anchor, a length of chain, and a length of twisted nylon. The chain holds the rode (chain plus line) down so that the pull on the anchor is horizontal. Chain also withstands abrasion from coral and other hard bottoms much better than nylon. The nylon supplies the remaining length of rode and its elasticity absorbs surging from the waves.

Every anchor system needs chain but how much? Boating catalogs offer made-up rodes consisting of 100 feet of nylon and 4 feet of chain. Why only 4 feet? Because chain costs ten times as much as nylon.

Don't shortchange yourself. The cruisers I interviewed didn't. Many liveaboards don't carry hull insurance but put the money into bigger anchors and more chain. The average amount of chain on their primary anchors was a staggering 115 feet, although 26% had only 20 to 25 feet, and 16% used all-chain rodes of 250 to 300 feet.

What is the total length of rode (chain plus line) on your primary anchor?

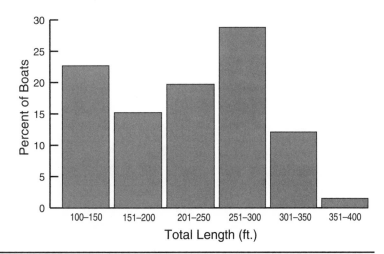

The average total length of rode was 240 feet. Assuming an average scope (defined on page 73) of 5.8, the average boat was prepared to anchor in depths of up to 40 feet.

In three years I have never had to anchor in more than 30 feet. I have never used more than 150 feet of my 300-foot rode and line could be added to the rode if necessary.

How many anchors, including those for the dinghy, do you carry?

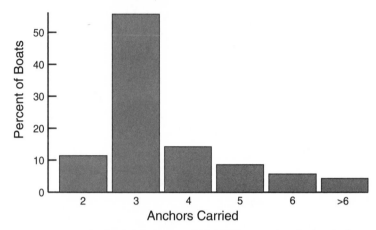

You can never have too many anchors, provided you have places to store them. Most production boats are set up to handle a single anchor on the foredeck. There is, if you are lucky, a single bow roller and a single chain locker. Because cruising boats encounter two-anchor situations so often, they should have rollers and chain lockers for two anchors in the bow.

Most of the boats carried at least three anchors, not that they weren't looking for more. You should see what happens in an anchorage when a novice abandons an anchor he can't raise. You'd think Blackbeard the Pirate had just jettisoned a chest of gold!

Do you have and have you ever used either a drogue or a sea anchor?

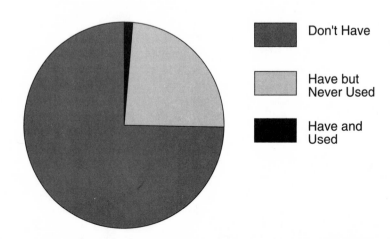

I've always been struck by the number of articles I've seen in sailing magazines about the proper use of sea anchors and drogues in storms at sea. I've never owned a sea anchor, and never known anyone who had used one, so my curiosity was peeked about the experiences of the cruisers.

A single cruiser had, in fact, used a sea anchor in a storm. It didn't work. He no longer carries it. Twenty-five percent have a sea anchor aboard but have never had occasion to use it. Most were gifts from family and friends who had read the same terrifying articles I had about storms at sea.

Defining "anchor scope" as the ratio of rode out to the distance from deck to bottom:

1. What scope do you use under average conditions?

2. What is the minimium overnight scope you would consider using under the ideal conditions of no wind and no current?

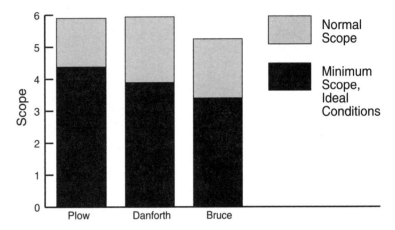

Anchor scope is defined as the ratio of length of rode deployed to the vertical distance from point of attachment (chock or roller) to the bottom. For example, if you anchor in 12 feet of water, your bow roller is 4 feet above the waterline, and you let out 80 feet of rode, your scope is 80÷(12 + 4) = 5, usually stated as "five to one."

Most sailors get into a habit of using the same scope, which I defined as their *normal scope.* Occasionally, you will find yourself in an extremely popular and tight anchorage where there is reason to use as small a scope as you dare. I defined *minimum scope* as that which they would not go below when anchoring overnight, even if there were zero wind, zero current, and no change forecasted.

Normal scope averaged 5.8. *Minimum scope* averaged 4.2.

Having read somewhere that *normal scope* for rodes with minimum chain should be seven and for all-chain rodes four, I expected to find a correlation between length of chain on the primary anchor and scope. There wasn't.

Average *normal scope* for less than 25 feet of chain was 5.63 and for more than 150 feet of chain was 5.60. Similar results were found for *minimum scope*: less than 25 feet of chain was 3.86 and more than 150 feet of chain was 4.10.

Many made an important point about the use of minimum scope. The procedure for minimum scope anchoring is to pay out normal scope, set the anchor by backing down at full power, then shortening the rode to minimum scope.

That made a lot of sense to me, since I found it nearly impossible to get an anchor to dig in at all using minimum scope, but nearly impossible to break loose later, even with a scope of as little as 2.

Overall, what percentage of time do you use two anchors instead of only one?

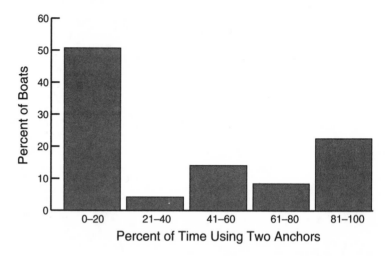

A personal experience sets the tone for the one- versus two-anchor question. During my first year on the ICW, I was still in the novice anchoring stage, when every anchorage presented a new twist. Since good anchorages are spread about 40 miles apart, which is the average daily distance most boats travel on the ICW, boats seem to travel in packs. My pack was plagued by a Teuton in leather shorts who shall go nameless. This fellow was the greenest sailor in the pack, but he apparently felt he had mastered the science of anchoring. Unfortunately, he always got underway, among much rattling and banging about, before sunrise and so was always the first to the next anchorage.

Now, it is a nautical custom that the first boat in an anchorage sets the style for all the others. Boats on one anchor swing a wide arc, with a radius equal to the rode deployed. Boats with two anchors, set 180 degrees apart off the bow, swing around the midpoint, as if they were on a mooring. In a big anchorage, it doesn't much matter which style is used, but mixing styles results in havoc.

Recovering two anchors is at least twice as difficult as recovering one, so it was with dismay that we would find him every evening, loud hailer in hand, directing us here and there with the instruction, *"Zwei anchor; zwei anchor!"*

I was about fed up and looking for a way to evade the manic Teuton, when in cruised an unfamiliar boat. When the sleek 50-foot craft from England had coasted up to a point abeam of the Teuton, the singlehander sauntered to the bow, let go the hook, backed down, and disappeared below.

"Zwei anchor! Zwei anchor!" intoned the flailing self-appointed harbormaster, at which the Brit popped his head from the hatch and said, "No thanks, old chap."

Most sailors prefer using single anchors—usually their trusty plows. The single anchor works as long as tidal currents aren't strong and reversing, and as long as the wind isn't predicted to switch overnight. As long as everyone in the anchorage is on a single anchor, all boats swing in unison and harmony.

If currents are strong and reversing, as they are in the Bahamas, then two anchors off the bow are preferred (thus the term *Bahamian moor*).

The cruisers balked at my simple-minded questioning.

"What percent of the time do I use two anchors *where*?" they insisted. Although the overall average was 37%, I'm sure it would have broken down better as: Bahamas, 90%; elsewhere, 10%.

Do you have, or would you like to have, an anchor windlass (anchors 35 pounds or over)?

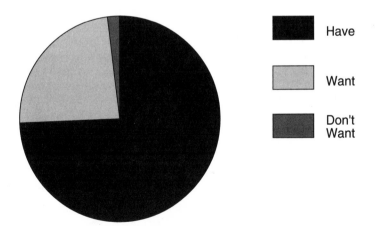

Have

Want

Don't Want

An anchor windlass multiplies your pull on the anchor rode, just as a winch does on a sheet or halyard. It's desirability should be proportional to the weight of the anchor. The windlass has further utility, independent of anchor weight. It secures the anchor by grabbing the chain, and it can be used to kedge off from the bow.

On those boats whose primary anchors weighed 35 pounds or more, 98% either had or desired a windlass. When the anchor weighed less than 35 pounds, 69% still found a windlass desirable.

*Do you always con-
sider the state and
range of the tides
when setting an
anchor?*

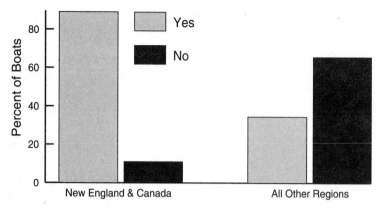

When calculating the length of rode to pay out on an
anchor, the skipper needs to take into account the fact
that the depth of water varies with the tide. I asked
whether the skipper always plugged the state and range
of tide into the scope equation. I was not surprised when
89% of those from New England, where the tide ranges
from 6 to 20 feet, said they did so. Only 35% of the skip-
pers from other areas paid attention to the tide.

*Upon entering a
crowded harbor at
sunset, you note sev-
eral substantial-
looking moorings
that you guess
belong to boats
away on cruises.
Would you take one
of the moorings, or
would you anchor?*

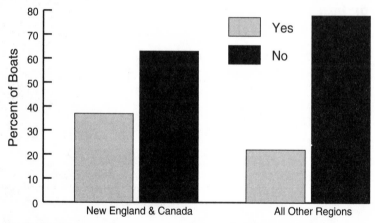

Seventy-three percent said they would not pick up a mooring, unless they knew what was on the bottom. Quite a few
distinguished between New England and other areas. In
New England one is often invited—even expected—to pick
up any mooring which hasn't been claimed by sunset. Of
course you may be awakened at midnight by the owner,
but at least it is not considered bad form.

In other areas it may be considered presumptuous to
pick up someone else's mooring, and the words might not
be so polite. The cruisers were not too concerned with
formalities, however. They just trusted their anchors a lot
more than what they couldn't see.

How many docklines (including former halyards, sheets, and the like) do you have aboard?

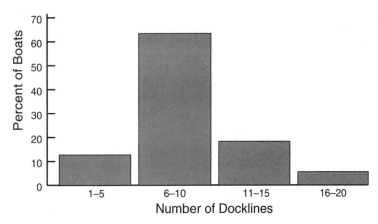

"What do you consider a dockline?" was the usual response. Sailors are reluctant to throw away anything that looks like rope and is more than 2 feet long. After a few years, the docklines on many boats are mostly old, running rigging. The average number of "docklines" carried was nine. One boat had 20!

How many fenders or bumpers do you carry aboard?

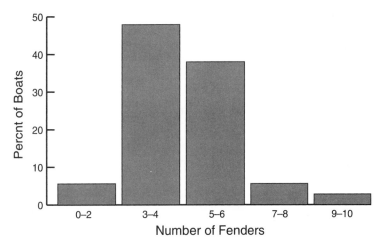

Fenders, or bumpers, take up space. They also can't be salvaged from some other use and are expensive. The average number of four was just about what was required.

Fender boards are horizontal planks use to fend a boat off pilings. In New England tidal ranges are large, and docks usually float up and down with the tide, so fender boards are not needed.

Except in New England and Georgia, tidal ranges on the U.S. East Coast are on the order of 1 to 2 feet, so fixed piers are often used. That calls for fender boards between a pair of fenders and the piles. Sixty-three percent of the boats carried at least one fender board.

10. Underway

Don't you think we should play it safe? It's only an hour to low tide.

Introduction

Considering the range of investment in the cruising boats—from an upgraded 22-foot daysailer to an 85-foot motorsailer once belonging to John Wayne—I am struck by the similarity of cruising lifestyles. When traveling the ICW, the boats seem like a flock of migrating geese all going about the same speed, making the same daily distances, and plopping down for the night in the same places.

Even the amount of disposable income makes little difference in the lifestyles. One cruiser's shorts came from Brooks Brothers, another's from K Mart; one dinghy is powered by a 15-hp Mercury, another by a 1.2-hp Sears Gamefisher; one boat has a microwave, another a camp stove. But the experience is all the same.

While sitting on a well-traveled 22-foot boat, whose only light was a portable fluorescent camp light and whose refrigerator was a sixpack hung over the side, the owner peered over his can of Milwaukee's Best and said, "Folks, it doesn't get any better than this!"

When cruising, how many nautical miles per day do you average?

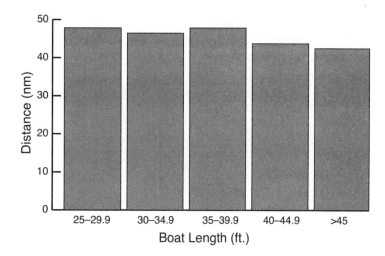

Don't imagine you need a large boat to go cruising. There was little correlation between size of boat and average daily distance. In fact, the boats under 30 feet averaged 10% greater distance than the boats over 40 feet! The overall average distance was 46 nautical miles, or 53 statute miles.

When cruising, how many hours per day do you average underway?

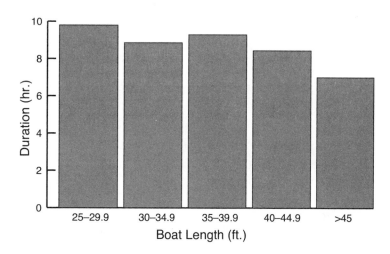

With lesser hull speed, smaller boats have to get underway earlier and put in longer days in order to do the same distance as larger boats.

Those under 30 feet put in an average of 9.8 hours from hook up to hook down. Those on boats over 40 feet spent an average of 8.4 hours underway. Half of the time difference is due to the fact that the smaller boats went greater distances.

What average daily speed made good do you use in planning a cruise?

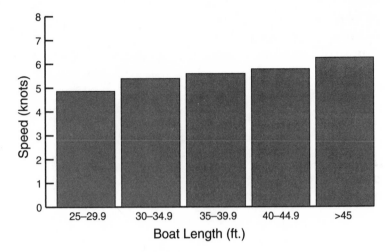

When the crew asks, "What time do we have to get underway tomorrow?" the navigator or captain goes through the following thought process:

1. how many miles is it to the next anchorage;
2. miles ÷ average speed made good = hours;
3. time of sunset (alternatively, cocktail hour) – hours = time to get underway.

The one fixed number in the equation is average speed made good. Not to be confused with hull speed, it is the speed that makes the captain happy considering engine rpm, fuel efficiency, prop vibration, etc. It also allows for getting out of the anchorage, bridge delays, a possible grounding, and getting into the next anchorage.

For boats under 30 feet, the speeds made good averaged 4.86 knots and for boats over 40 feet, 5.78 knots.

What is the longest (in nautical miles) non-stop passage you have made in this boat?

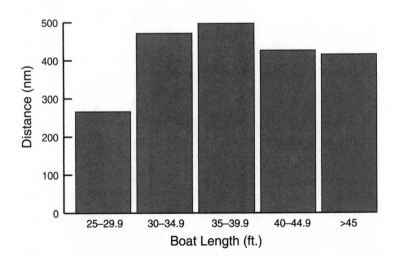

You might expect that larger boats, having greater fuel capacities, would make longer passages. Surprise! Although boats in the 35- to 39.9-foot range made the longest average trips (497 nm), boats 30 to 34.9 feet beat both boats 40 to 44.9 feet and boats 45 feet and up.

The longest passage in each group was: 975 nm (25 to 29.9 feet); 3,000 nm (30 to 34.9 feet); 1,200 nm (35 to 39.9 feet); 1,000 nm (40 to 44.9 feet); and 700 nm (45 feet and up).

What is the longest (in days) non-stop passage you have made in this boat?

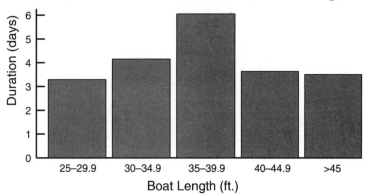

More interesting as a test of endurance is the longest passage in days at sea. Again, the 35- to 39.9-foot boats stayed out the longest times, averaging 6.0 days.

Don't get the idea that the boats surveyed were "ocean cruisers." Seventeen percent had never exceeded either 100 nm or one day.

Do you sometimes sail overnight?

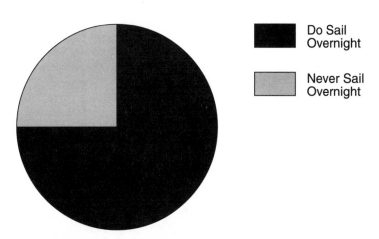

It's hard to exceed 100 nm unless you're willing to sail in the dark. Only tugboat captains would attempt the shoaled ICW at night, so sailing overnight means sailing in the ocean or large bodies such as Chesapeake Bay. Seventy-five percent sailed overnight at least occasionally.

***How many times do
you expect to go
aground in the next
twelve months?***

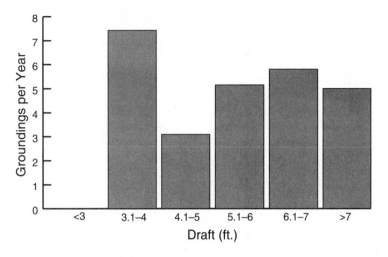

Having learned to be careful in phrasing the question about groundings, I finally settled on, "Never mind what you intend to do or feel competent to do, how many times do you expect to go aground next year?"

To a person from the rockbound coast of Maine, the answers were at first shocking. Hitting a granite ledge at cruising speed will most certainly ruin your day, if not your pocketbook. But after running the ICW and the fluffy calcareous sands of the Bahamas, I have become much more cavalier. After running aground my first thought is usually, "Well, at least now the bottom is clean."

The average of yearly groundings was five. I found it curious and amusing that the greatest frequency of groundings was for boats with the shallowest drafts. I can only conclude that grounding has more to do with care than it does with draft.

***Which of the follow-
ing "disasters" have
you experienced?***

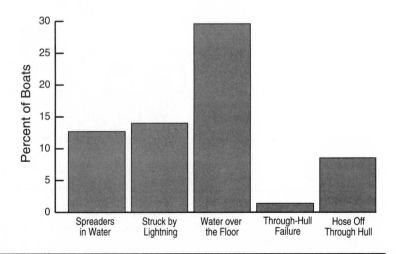

disasters

When family and friends hear you have lost your mind and plan to go sailing indefinitely, the first thing they picture is you gaunt and hollow-eyed, clinging to a bit of wreckage, and surrounded by shark fins.

Don't laugh! Several years ago a couple apparently struck a sleeping whale whose tail-jerk reaction stove a hole in their hull. Their rescue, after a month at sea, was the media story of the month. A friend of mine who knew I planned to go cruising, phoned in an obvious state of alarm. "How are you going to avoid running into whales?" he demanded.

"Funny, I was just thinking about how I might find some whales," I said.

Which brings us to the questions of knockdowns, lightning, and other "disasters."

knockdowns

Nine boats had been caught under full sail in a squall and had the tips of their spreaders in the water. Although scary as all get out, and although water will enter through any ports which have been left open, a sailboat has its maximum righting tendency in that position. Sailboats with closed decks do not sink by being knocked down. Dividing the total years of cruising by the number of knockdowns, the Mean Time Between Disasters (MTBD) was 31 years.

lightning

Ten boats had been struck by lightning. Although most had lost electronics to the marauding electrons, and several had suffered scorched sails and melted antennas, not a single crewmember was injured. MTBD was 28 years.

water above the floor-boards

Water can accumulate in the bilge in a number of ways: burying the rail with a leaky hull-deck joint; faulty stuffing box; disconnected engine cooling water hose; discharge hose which siphons when heeled. My boat took 150 gallons of seawater through an uncovered anchor hawsepipe while plowing through head seas.

Most of the time an automatic bilge pump will bail water as fast as it comes in. Occasionally, however, the bilge pump switch dies, or the pump becomes clogged, and the first hint you have that something is amiss is floating floor boards.

This "disaster" had happened to 21 boats. No boats sunk. The worst casualty was a box of videotapes that had to be thrown away. MTBD = 13 years.

through-hull failure

A single boat had experienced failure of a through hull. The bronze seacock had suffered so much electrolysis (electrical corrosion) that it simply packed it in and disintegrated. A routine inspection would have spotted the problem. The boat didn't sink and no one died. MTBD = 277 years.

hose off through hull

If you've ever had a marine survey performed on your boat, you've probably been lectured to install two new stainless hose clamps on every through hull hose. It's good advice. They only cost $1 apiece, and if one fails, the other will prevent disaster. Six of the cruisers hadn't double-clamped, and hoses had popped off. The result depends on the size of the hose and how the crew reacts to crisis. If it's a 2-inch hose, the location is difficult to access, and the crew panics, the boat could fill up and sink in 10 to 15 minutes. On the other hand, a cool head and a set of wood through-hull plugs will save the boat.

None of the six boats were lost. MTBD = 46 years.

Do you carry fire-arms (not including flare guns) aboard?

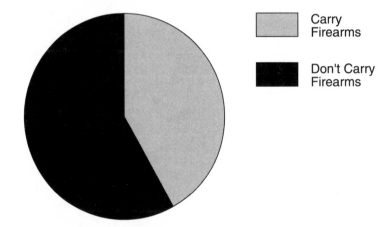

Carry Firearms

Don't Carry Firearms

Your friends will warn you about the pirates who lurk offshore, waiting to pillage and plunder your boat. If you tell them you're headed for South or Central America, they'll likely go berserk. Just tell them to forget the dozen murders they watched on American prime-time television the night before.

I have met many sailors from Canada and Europe who consider any major U.S. city more dangerous than any Caribbean Island.

A majority (58%) of the sailors did not feel they had to carry a gun. Some of the more common statements were:

> "If you're not sure you could kill another human being, don't carry a gun, because it will probably be used against you."

> "A flare gun looks like a gun, is legal everywhere, and will do as much damage as a handgun."

> "You are safer traveling in a group of unarmed boats than you are traveling alone, even if armed to the hilt."

Do you ever get seasick?

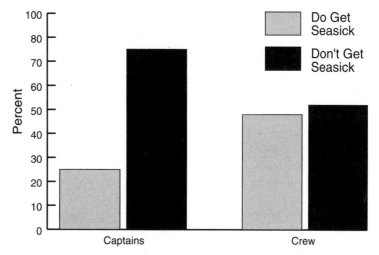

If you've ever been seasick (a near-death experience during which you wish someone would shoot you), you'll have to wonder why so many of the seasick-prone crews are still out there. The answer must lie in the fact that most have found preventatives, and that the alternative of not cruising is unthinkable.

The graph above shows a real difference between captains (usually men) and their crews (usually women). Only 25% of the captains get seasick, as compared to 48% of the crews. Two reasons occur to me:

1. You are less prone to *mal de mer* while at the helm. When steering you have the sensation that you are causing the motion of the boat rather than being passively tossed about. It also helps to watch the horizon as a reference level.

2. The captains are usually the prime movers. Someone who has experienced seasickness is less likely to think cruising is a nifty idea. The spouses may be going along with the captains' lifelong dreams of cruising.

(Males) What do you use to prevent seasickness?

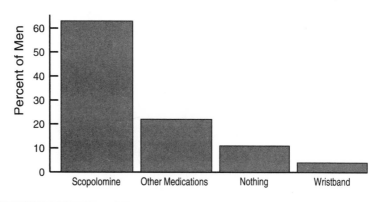

A comparison of what men and women do to prevent sea-sickness is striking. Of the 25% of men who get seasick, 63% use Scopolomine (the ear patch), 22% use various other medications, 11% macho it out with nothing, and 4% wear the wristband.

(Females) What do you use to prevent seasickness?

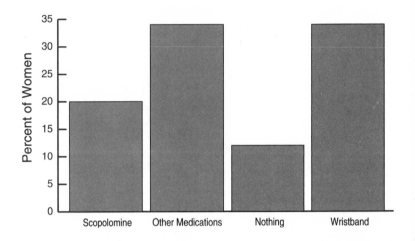

Of the seasick women, only 20% use the patch, 34% various medications, 34% the wristband, and 12% tough it out.

seasickness preventatives for men and women combined

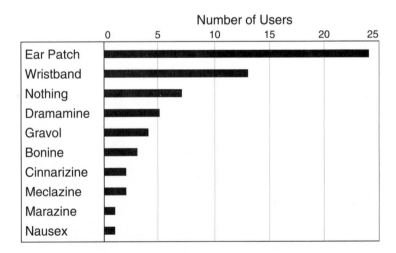

Overall, the patch was the most common preventative, followed by the wristband. The numbers of all users are shown above.

The ear patch stirred the most comment. Many said they had tried it but with unhappy results. Nearly all users suffered from dry mouth. A few had experienced disorientation, which they felt may have been due to mixing the patch with other medications such as blood pressure pills.

On the other hand, many of its proponents called the patch an absolute miracle. It is effective for up to a week, it produces no drowsiness, and often half a patch is enough.

My advice is to try the patch on land before you go to sea.

11. Skills

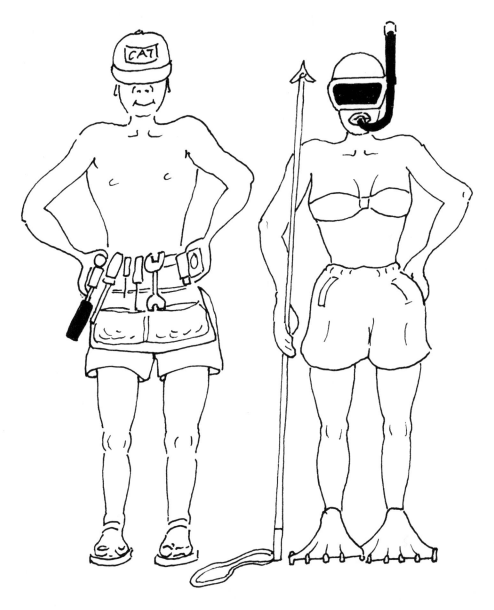

Tom and Mary Ann are ready for the biggest adventure of their lives.

Introduction

Nothing offered in college or high school will prepare you for a life afloat. Living aboard is a prime example of the "school of hard knocks." It's a school with open enrollment. Anyone can try. Within a semester you'll either quit and go home, or you will have gained a new level of confidence and will be looking forward to the next experience.

There are two kinds of liveaboards:

1. A small number have the resources to pay someone else to solve all of their problems. If they go aground, they call a towing service; if their engine coughs, they call a diesel mechanic; if their radio quits, they buy a new one.

2. The majority are barely getting by. If they go aground, they kedge off or wait for the tide; if their engine quits, they get a crash course in diesel mechanics from kibbitzing with their friends; if their radio quits, they get out the volt-ohm meter and the soldering iron.

I think the second group has more fun. Even if its not all fun, the sense of confidence gained from the sea school of hard knocks cannot be purchased at any price.

There are several widely available courses you can take on land before setting out on your new life. My own education began with the introductory boating course offered by the U.S. Power Squadrons. A similar course is offered by the Coast Guard Auxiliary. Both are available in hundreds of locations, so finding one should be no problem.

Taking the course lowers boat insurance premiums by 15%. Since I planned to live aboard for at least 10 years, and since my insurance costs about $1,200 per year, I estimated that attending the 10-week course would save me $1,800—not bad for a $15 investment in the course materials!

Like Water Rat in *The Wind in the Willows*, I had been "messing about in boats" most of my life. It was thus with smug anticipation that I sat down among all of the first-time boaters to take the "preliminary exam." I figured to score at least 95, more likely 98.

My score was 68. I knew how to tie a dozen knots. I could name every part of a complex sailboat. But how could I be expected to know what percent of a boat's weight should be on a trailer hitch? How was I supposed to know how big a fire extinguisher a 26-foot boat should carry, or whether one should close the hatches when taking on gasoline?

Well, after recovering my pride and burning the midnight oil, I aced the final exam! After oiling the gears in my out-of-school-for-20-years brain, I was on a roll. I enrolled in the American Red Cross's Advanced First Aid, obtained Novice and Technician Amateur Radio licenses, and with luminous intensity, finally obtained a Coast Guard 50-ton Master and Mate of Inland Waters License with Auxiliary Sail Endorsement.

My experience proved not to be unique. You'll find that a high percentage of liveaboards have attended many formal courses.

Which of the following skills or licenses are possessed by at least one member of your crew?

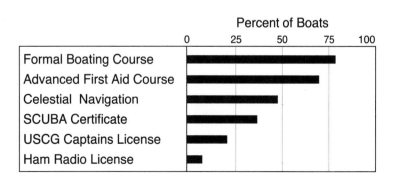

boating courses:
Power Squadron, or
C.G. Auxiliary

Seventy-nine percent had taken one of the introductory boating courses. Most had repeated my experience of signing up in order to reduce their insurance premiums by 15%, but finding, in the end, that they had learned more than they thought possible.

first aid

Seventy percent had taken an American Red Cross First Aid course that went beyond CPR. Many had been struck by the number of First Aid books directed at the cruiser. The covers generally resemble those of the little Red Cross first aid manuals; however, inside you'll find graphic pictures such as a leg being removed above the knee with a hack saw!

When I asked why one woman had taken an Emergency Medical Technician (EMT) course, she replied, "There ain't no 911 offshore, Honey!"

celestial navigation

If one were to cross an ocean, and if one's electronics were to fail, and if one happened to have a watch that kept incredibly good time, a sextant, and an up-to-date nautical almanac, then one could use celestial navigation to find one's position. The small likelihood of all of that happening does not come close to explaining why 48% of the cruisers had learned celestial. Most admitted they had never had occasion to use the skill. It simply represented the ultimate in sailing competence.

SCUBA certificate

A SCUBA certificate, without which you cannot rent SCUBA equipment or have a tank filled, can be had with the expenditure of a week's time and $200. Not being in the Caribbean should not stop you. Courses are offered in swimming pools all over the world. I was at first surprised that only 37% had a certificate. But after cruising and snorkeling the 10-foot depths of the Florida Keys and the Bahamas, I agreed with the majority that a snorkel, fins, mask, and a good set of lungs are all you need.

captain's license

Twenty-one percent of the "captains" also had a USCG captain's license or foreign equivalent. A few had taken the course just for its content (which is considerable and roughly equivalent to a tough college course), but most had entertained the idea of making money by either chartering their own boat or by delivering other boats.

The financial aspect was usually a big disappointment. A single charter experience disabused most of the notion that they could make money and have fun at the same time. When someone pays you several thousand big ones for a week of fun in the sun, they expect you to deliver. High winds, rough seas, fog, or other acts of God are no excuse. You quickly get the idea of what it must be like to be a prostitute or a politician.

The delivery business also proved disappointing to many. They quickly discovered that yacht deliveries are made by a few captains who are plugged into delivery agencies or into an established list of clients. In every popular boating center, there are two captains for every boat.

amateur (ham) radio license

A General Class Amateur Radio license is one of the most coveted and least achieved dreams of the cruiser. Imagine, as all cruisers do while waiting in line for the pay phone, chatting away with your friends back home without leaving the nav station and without paying AT&T a cent!

Then why do only 8% of the cruisers have ham licenses? After all, you can now get a license without learning the dreaded Morse Code, and we've all seen pictures of six-year-olds who have mastered the international airwaves. The reason is that *actually talking* on any of the *useful* frequency bands still requires receiving Morse Code at 13 words per minute. At five characters per word and four beeps per character, it translates into 13 gazillion beeps per second. To a child who has only been talking for a few years, this is a game. To a 50-year-old brain, besotted with cheap red wine for too many of those years, it seems like absolute gibberish.

Of the six cruisers who had ham licenses, four were still chasing the coveted General Class license, so that they could legally talk on their expensive rigs.

Which of the following operations could be performed by someone on your crew?

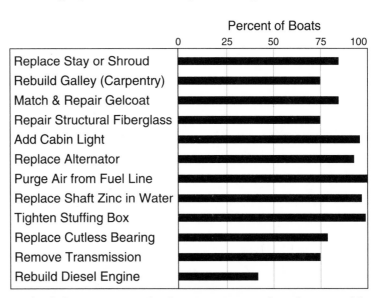

I asked the cruisers whether anyone on their boat could perform each of twelve common maintenance or repair jobs, ranging in difficulty from purging the air out of the diesel fuel line to completely rebuilding the engine.

Compared to a similar number of flatlanders, the cruisers were do-it-yourselfers *par excellence.* Most could do every task I threw at them, except rebuild a diesel. After a few affirmative replies, I felt most were barely restraining themselves from saying, "Of course I can—why, can't you?"

In case you find this distressing, let me once again recount personal experience. When I first moved aboard, I could rebuild the galley, add a cabin light, purge air from the diesel fuel line, replace the zincs on the shaft, and tighten the stuffing box. Now, after three years aboard, I have learned how to do all of the remaining tasks, except rebuild the diesel.

How did I suddenly come by this knowledge? Something broke and fellow boaters showed me how. After one showed me how to replace my cutless bearing, I asked how I might repay him, and he replied, "You can repay me by doing for the next guy what I just did for you and what someone else once did for me."

Do you rate yourself as a strong, weak, or non-swimmer?

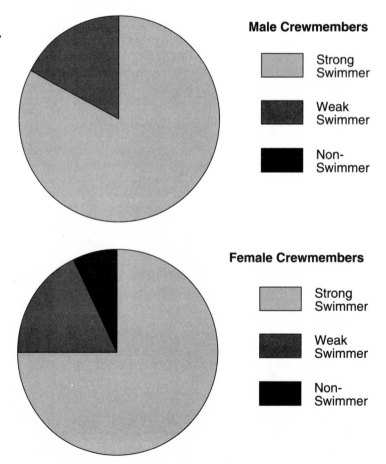

Male Crewmembers

Strong Swimmer

Weak Swimmer

Non-Swimmer

Female Crewmembers

Strong Swimmer

Weak Swimmer

Non-Swimmer

A strong swimmer is defined as one who could swim a mile, and a weak swimmer is defined as one who could make it around the boat. I wish I had added average swimmer, because that was what most wanted to reply.

Because it was most often the males' idea to go cruising, it was not surprising that all of the men could swim, but that 7% of the women could not.

12. Safety

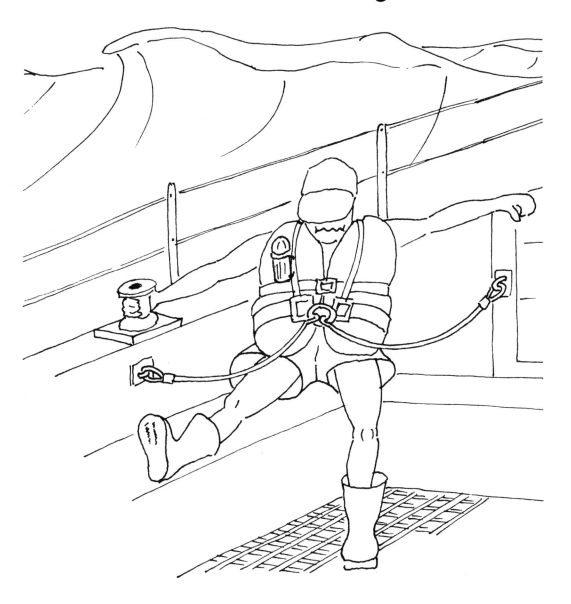

What do you mean, "What about lunch?"

Introduction

The analysis of the safety responses left me with mixed feelings. On the one hand, I was dismayed at the lack of safety equipment on about half of the boats. On the other hand, I was impressed by the total acceptance and rigorous use of safety harnesses.

Without exception the cruisers' attitude toward safety was, "You can't be lost if you don't go overboard, and if you do go overboard, you probably won't be found."

This attitude explains why so many of the boats lacked man-overboard (MOB) and abandon-ship equipment, but had and extensively used safety harnesses designed to keep crewmembers on board.

Have you ever practiced and/or experienced a man-overboard accident?

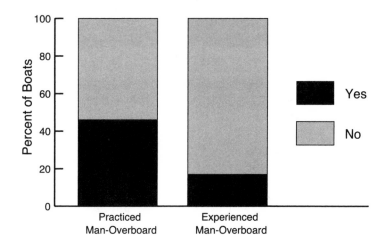

Cruisers are not young hotshot racers selected for their superb physical condition. They are typically middle-aged couples who have moved onto their boats, after lives spent in office and home.

Fewer than half of the crews had ever practiced recovery of a person who had fallen overboard. Those who had practiced MOB admitted that getting a waterlogged crewmember aboard was far more difficult than they had imagined.

As a result of their MOB experiments, all had determined to never let anyone ever fall overboard while underway, and some had installed permanent fold-down ladders or steps on their transoms.

In which of the following situations do you always wear a PFD/safety harness?

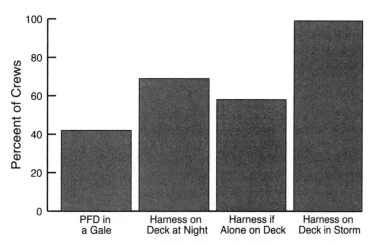

As required by law, all of the boats carried personal flotation devices (PFDs) for all aboard. Most, however, regarded PFDs as PIBs (pains in the butt) and would wear them only if abandoning ship.

There are now very stylish inflatable PFDs that look and feel more like windbreakers than life jackets, but few cruisers expressed interest in these either.

On the other hand, safety harnesses were totally accepted. A good safety harness, a short tether, and a taut jackline (line running from cockpit to bow to which the harness tether is clipped) will keep a harnessed crewmember aboard, even if knocked unconscious by a flying boom. At the very worst, the MOB will find him or herself being dragged alongside the boat.

Each crewmember was asked what he or she would wear if required to leave the cockpit and go to the foredeck under various conditions:

- In a gale, only 42% would wear a PFD, but 97% would wear a harness.

- In good conditions, and being the only person on deck, none would wear a PFD, but 58% would put on the harness.

- In good conditions underway at night with other crew watching, 14% would wear a PFD, but 70% would wear a harness.

Which of the following safety equipment do you carry aboard?

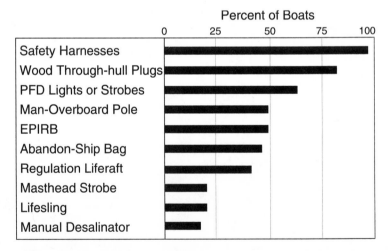

safety harnesses

As already discussed, 97% of the boats carried individual safety harnesses. Most carried a harness for each member, plus one for each guest so that they could be individually fitted and left on between watches.

wood through-hull plugs

Eighty-two percent carried softwood plugs to hammer into failed through hulls or hoses. The plugs are available in sets of four, sized to fit any through hull up to a 2-inch cockpit drain. There is no excuse for not having a set since they cost about the same as a six-pack of beer.

PFD lights or strobe

Sixty-three percent carried either small, clip-on, water-proof lights or strobes. The lights are designed to be pinned to a PFD or strapped to an arm, which makes a MOB much more visible at night.

man-overboard pole

Half of the boats carried MOB poles. The pole consists of a flag on a tall, reflective spar which is weighted to float upright and mark the position of a MOB (or at least the place where it was thrown overboard), enabling the MOB to swim to the pole for a rescue rendezvous with the boat.

EPIRB

About half of the boats also carried EPIRBs, which may be manually or automatically actuated to signal the location of the distressed vessel. Depending on the class of the EPIRB, the signals will be picked up by either coastal stations, passing aircraft, or transiting satellites.

The sailors had mixed feelings about EPIRBs. They had heard of dramatic, midocean rescues effected with the devices, but they had also heard of the discouraging Coast Guard tests in which many of the units failed to transmit a signal strong enough to be received by satellite. The situation for new EPIRBs has been rectified by more stringent specifications and more rigorous testing, but those with existing units are left wondering whether anyone will ever hear their calls for help.

A lot of the sailors expressed the feeling that the money would be better spent on an extra hand-held VHF and plenty of extra batteries (see below).

abandon-ship bag

If one has a certified liferaft, it will contain a few basic life-support aids, such as canned water, food rations, first aid kit, signal mirror, knife, etc.

Many who don't have one of the expensive liferafts (and some who have, as well) have put together abandon-ship bags which can be quickly grabbed as the ship goes down. The contents of the bag depend on one's preferences and pocketbook. Common items are the ones listed above, plus space blankets, pocket AM/FM radios, tools, and books (the *Bible* and Steve Callahan's *Adrift* are very popular).

It is generally agreed that the most important item to carry is a hand-held VHF radio with which to signal passing ships. The chances of a ship seeing a liferaft are about 1%, but of hearing the radio about 90%, since ships at sea are required by international law to monitor channel 16. Make sure you carry either extra batteries or, even better, a small solar charger for the radio.

regulation liferaft	Slightly less than half (41%) had regulation liferafts. Most stated that they would either buy or rent one before crossing the ocean, but they felt the dangers of sailing only 50 miles from shore didn't warrant the several thousand dollar cost. Instead, they felt either towing or having aboard an inflated dinghy and an abandon ship bag with hand-held VHF was a better investment.
masthead strobe	The masthead strobe light, sold by several companies as part of a masthead tri-color navigation light, is an interesting safety option. On the one hand, its use is prohibited under international navigation rules because it might be confused with an aid to navigation. On the other hand, if you were to call the Coast Guard for assistance at night, one of the first questions they would ask is whether or not you have a strobe.
	When law conflicts with safety at sea, the rule most go by is, "in an emergency, anything goes."
"Lifesling"	The "Lifesling" is a patented system for retrieving and hoisting aboard a MOB. It consists of a flotation device deployed on a 150-foot line behind the boat. The boat maneuvers to put the line in the MOBs path. The MOB then slips the flotation band under his arms and is hauled in and hoisted aboard with a block and tackle.
	Everyone agrees it is a far better system than the classic rigid horseshoe of the past but only 20% of the boats had switched to date. Considering the short time the "Lifesling" has been on the market, that represents an impressive penetration of the market.
manual desalinator	Desalinators make fresh water from salt water by forcing water through a membrane which is permeable to pure water only. Both manual (about $500) and motor-driven ($2,000 to $3,000) versions are available, and at least one of the motor-driven units can be quickly disconnected to allow removal of the piston for manual use in an emergency.
	Those who can afford the larger, motor-driven units are beginning to install them for their main source of water. Few of the cruisers had purchased manual-only units. Of the 17% who had manual desalinators, at least three-quarters were the removable piston-type from motor-driven units.

13. Social/Personal

Arnie goes to all the parties.

Introduction

The personal questions were left until I felt I had penetrated my subjects' defenses. Even so, there were awkward moments as when I asked their ages. We had some laughs, and it helped that I was beyond the average age.

This section of the survey, better than any other, gives an idea of the cruising lifestyle. The cruising life has little to do with the size of your boat; rather, whether you and your mate are both having fun. It has less to do with the size of your bank account; rather, the number of weeks per night you socialize with other cruisers.

This chapter provides an inside view of the armchair sailor's favorite fantasy—living on a boat.

(Male adults) What is your present age?

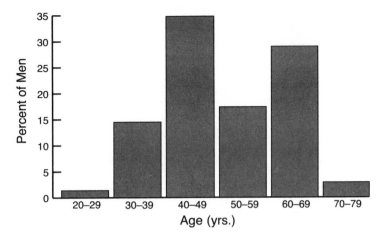

You know something is up when you look at the age distribution of adult males. Two peaks jump out:

- ages 40 to 49 (35%)
- ages 60 to 69 (29%)

The first peak is the age of mid-life crisis when a male asks himself, "Is this all there is?" There's no need for me to digress on the nature of mid-life crises; I'll merely state that it is apparently the most common reason male cruisers are out there.

The second peak is the retirees. They had been planning their liveaboard retirement for 10 or 20 years. Many retired in their late fifties, anxious to cruise as long as their health permitted.

(Female adults) What is your present age?

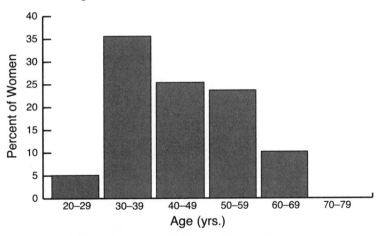

The age distribution of adult females is radically different from that of the males. There is no peak at 60 to 69, but there is a large one at 30 to 39. While there were quite a few mature couples who were sharing a lifelong dream,

I'm afraid there were more cases in which wife number one had opted out of her husband's mad fantasy, to be replaced by a younger and more adventuresome wife number two. This is verified by the overall average ages: males, 49.5; females, 36.7.

The average age difference would have been more striking if it weren't for several 40-ish female captains who had reversed the tables by selecting male partners in their 20s.

How many years have you been boating, including small boats?

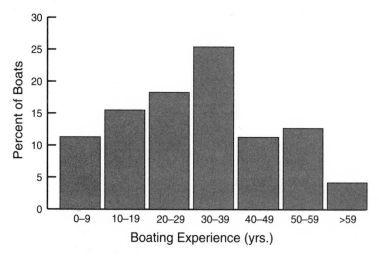

The notion of going boating had not erupted from nowhere. The average number of years spent "messing about in boats" was 30. Considering the ages of the boaters, their boating experiences must have started in childhood.

For most, however, the experience, up to the point of moving aboard, was on much smaller boats or boats belonging to friends. Most could not have afforded their present boats before they became their primary residences.

How many years have you been living aboard your boat?

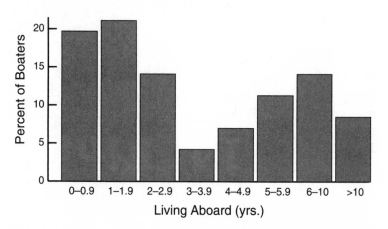

Years living aboard also shows a pair of peaks: 0 to 2.9 years, and 6 to 10 years. The shorter span represents those who set aside money and a year or two of their lives to go cruising. Many still own homes and automobiles back home. Most *will* return to the worlds they left behind, but a few will find ways to extend their live-aboard lifestyles to the rest of their active lives.

The second group have succeeded in making living aboard work for them. Typically, they are no longer encumbered by home, automobile, dependent children, or other responsibilities. They are gypsies of the sea, coming and going as they like, and stopping to make money only when needed. They will continue until illness forces them back to land.

How many total nautical miles have you cruised in your own boat(s)?

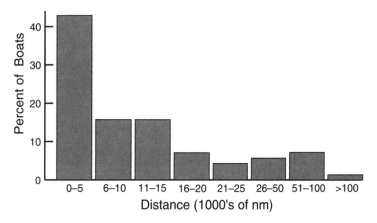

These cruisers were no greyhounds of the sea. Only six had logged more than 50,000 nm. About half had logged less than 5,000 nm in all of their boats (all the boats they had owned, including the present one). The overall average distance was 14,900 nm.

The typical cruiser logged about 2,000 nm per year in his seasonal migrations. As discussed under anchoring, an average of one day per week is spent underway but six on the hook.

(Males) If living on land is a five, how do you rate living on a boat on a scale of 1 to 10?

I had more fun with this question than with any other. It was one part of a four-part question:

1. how do you (male) rate the cruising life;
2. what was your (male) prior expectation;
3. how do you (female) rate the cruising life;
4. what was your (female) prior expectation.

By my definition five or above meant the cruising life was at least as good as the life they had left on land. Not a single male gave cruising less than a five.

Seventy percent rated cruising as eight or better, and 22% gave it a full 10 ("it doesn't get any better than this").

The males' prior expectations were nearly identical to present ratings. The present averaged 8.2 while the prior expectation averaged 8.3.

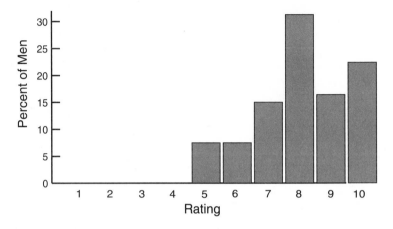

(Females) If living on land is a five, how do you rate living on a boat on a scale of 1 to 10?

More women than men rated cruising nine or above. Their male mates were often surprised at the enthusiasm with which they had adapted to life afloat.

A second group concentrated at seven, just below the average of 8.1. To put their feelings into words, these women found cruising fun, but had a few reservations, such as rough weather and a shortage of water for bathing.

A third small (5.2%) group ranked cruising as less desirable than life on land. They would go home tomorrow, if their husbands would too, and had come to humor their husbands.

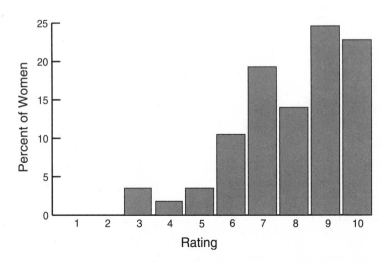

What time do you rise (first person)?

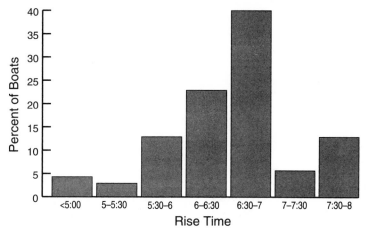

Sailors are more in tune with nature than the average person. Living in very small spaces, they live out of doors as much as possible. When below, they still open the hatches as much as possible (remember, they are in endless summer). They are not cut off from nature, as are landlubbers behind their drapes and tall buildings. As the graph above shows, they rise with the sun, averaging 6:40 A.M.

What time are the lights out on your boat?

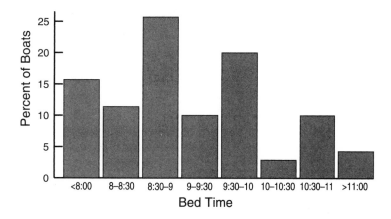

After saying that sailors rise with the sun, it is still a shock to see how they set with the sun as well. One in six are in bed before 8 P.M.! More than half go to bed by 9 P.M. Only one in 25 get to see the 11 P.M. news. The average time spent sleeping is nine hours and 35 minutes!

How does one account for this catlike behavior? Are they bored? Do they have no television or reading lights? Are they antisocial? No, none of these are true.

As for boredom, one said, "Cruising is the only lifestyle I know where you begin the day with nothing to do, but never get time to finish."

We've already seen that 73% of the boats have televisions. Yet, when you look around an anchorage at 9 P.M., over half of the lights are out, and when you have guests for dinner, the yawns begin at 8 P.M.

I think it is simply because the life of the sailor is more like the life of a cat. It is more natural and has fewer stresses. Without the frenetic, caffeinated stimulations of the city and suburb, man reverts into his natural animal state and moves into synchronism with the sun.

(Males) Is living aboard more or less stressful than living on land?

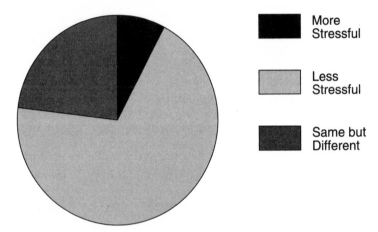

Most agreed that the cruising life is less stressful. Only 8% of the males felt more stressed now than before moving aboard. Twenty-three percent said there was the same amount of stress, but it was of a different sort. Cruising stresses are more natural, of your own making, and not unhealthy. Land stresses are often imposed from the outside and, if unresolved, detrimental to your health.

(Females) Is living aboard more or less stressful than living on land?

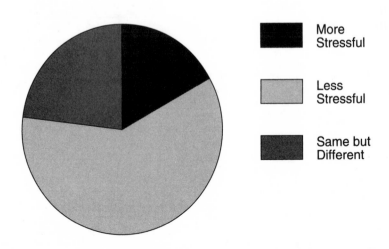

The women generally agreed with the men, except that a few more felt cruising more stressful. When questioned further, most said the stress was due to lack of sailing experience and manifested itself as fear in uncertain situations.

One woman aptly expressed the difference between sea and land stresses. "On land I'm just generally stressed all the time. At sea the stress is a roller coaster—when I'm scared, I'm afraid for my life, but when I'm mellow, I've never been so content in my life."

(Males) Since moving aboard, have you gained or lost weight?

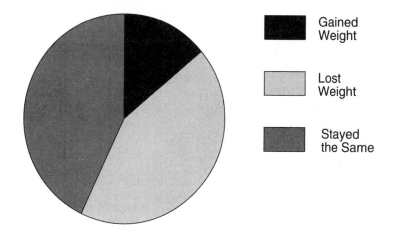

Gained Weight

Lost Weight

Stayed the Same

Weight Watchers, listen up! Forty-three percent of the men claim to have lost (and kept off) weight since moving aboard. Only 14% had gained weight.

(Females) Since moving aboard, have you gained or lost weight?

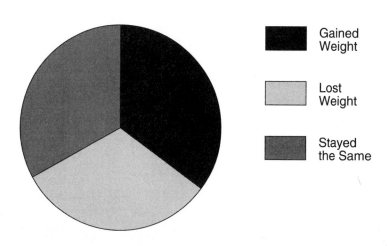

Gained Weight

Lost Weight

Stayed the Same

The women were not quite as successful in losing weight, but about as many lost (32%) as gained (35%).

Ignoring the inevitable effects of age, are you in better or worse overall physical condition since moving aboard?

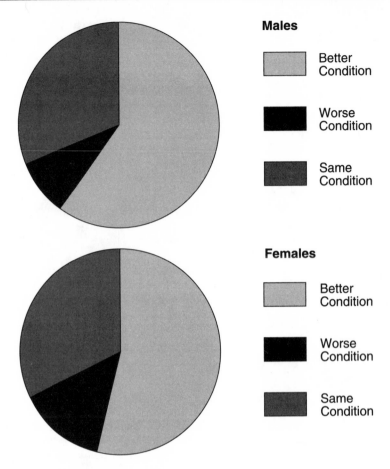

Males

Better Condition

Worse Condition

Same Condition

Females

Better Condition

Worse Condition

Same Condition

Even if one doesn't lose weight on a boat, the weight will become better distributed. Sixty percent of the men and 54% of the women felt that cruising had put them into better physical condition.

How many people would a manufacturer or broker claim your boat could sleep?

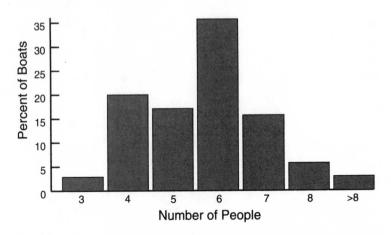

According to real estate agents, the ideal house today has four bedrooms, three baths, and a two-car garage. Reading boat advertisements, one would think the ideal cruising boat would sleep six and have two heads.

Maybe they're talking about charter boats. The cruisers, whose average number aboard was only 2.1, clucked and chuckled when I asked how many their boats were advertised to sleep. Only two of the boats could sleep less than four, and a significant number could sleep seven or more. The average was 5.8.

What is the average number of people sleeping on your boat?

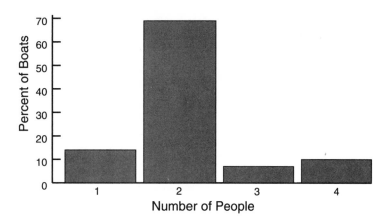

When a boat had more than one "stateroom," the second had invariably been converted to *le garage* (a space looking as if it had been packed by a trash compactor). One sailor had created a database on his laptop computer which listed the location and depth of burial of every item on his boat.

How many weeks per year do you have guests sleeping aboard?

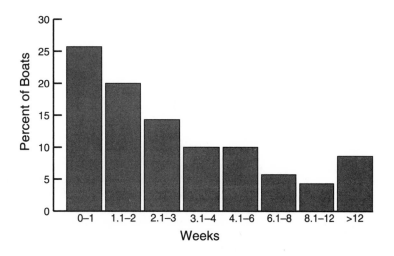

During "guest weeks" *le garage* is emptied with the contents being stashed in various locations, such as the cockpit, in every corner, and the guest's automobile. The number of those weeks averaged 4.2. About half limited visits to two or fewer weeks. A few, notably divorced parents having summer custody, had guests for eight or more weeks.

On average, how many nights per week do you eat dinner in a restaurant?

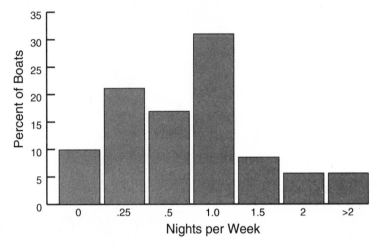

The average number of restaurant dinners per week was slightly less than one. Nearly a third ate out no more than once per month. Only 10% ate out two or more nights per week.

How many nights per week do you socialize?

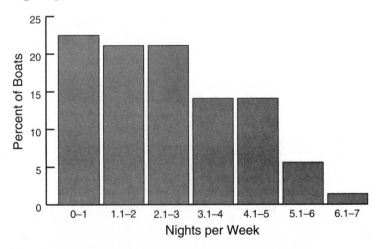

The cruisers may not step out on the town very much, but in the evening they sure dinghy over to other boats. The average couple socialized three out of seven nights. Twenty-two percent were relative recluses at one or less night per week, and an equal number were out at least four nights.

Boat galleys are small, so preparing dinner for four is a chore, and dinner for six is a feat. It is customary for the guests to bring either hors d'oeuvres or dessert.

In the Bahamas cocktail parties are often much more than that. Each of three or more couples brings a substantial hors d'oeuvre, and the resulting smorgasbord more often than not serves as dinner.

(All adults) Do you carry clothing suitable for attending a wedding or funeral?

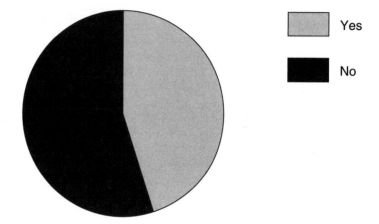

Yes

No

I asked the first few interviewees whether they had suits and dresses aboard. This was met with knee-slapping guffaws. I learned to tone it down to "clothing suitable for attending a wedding or funeral."

"Whose?" was the inevitable reply.

Anyway, fewer than half carried fancy clothes by their own definitions. One woman held up one leg of a pair of pantyhose and said, "I hope the only use I'll ever have for this sucker is straining diesel."

After the first year, my wife and I sent home our mildewed suits and dresses. When invited to the wedding of a dear friend's daughter in Washington, D.C., the best we could muster were a dog-eared blue blazer and chinos with only a hint of a grease stain for me and a wrinkled pantsuit for my wife. Her nails were split, and I had a patch of oozing sun poisoning on my cheek. At the reception, people in $500 suits, $200 shoes, and $100 hairdos kept staring at us. Feeling conspicuous, we sat at a table attempting to hide our shoes, pants, and hands. Finally, a friend came over and said, "Do you see how envious everyone is? You look great!"

What pets do you have aboard?

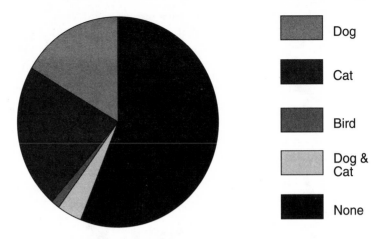

Dog

Cat

Bird

Dog & Cat

None

Pets make great boating companions. I'm convinced they love the boating life as much as humans. Twenty-three percent of the boats had one or more cats, and 17% had a dog. Only one had a parrot.

Pets on board can be treated exactly as they would be on land. Contrary to what you may have read, animals on boats do not need claws. When the going gets rough, they wedge themselves into their personal secure spots, which can be a bookcase, behind the settee cushions, in a knitting bag, or in your berth.

Cats have their litter boxes, usually kept in the shower stall or cockpit. Dogs are usually rowed ashore morning and evening, although I've seen a few dogs who are toilet trained, so to speak. I watched one dog jump overboard, swim to shore, do his thing, swim back, and climb into the dinghy. There he stayed until dry, whereupon he jumped back on the boat. Other dogs have been trained to pee in the scuppers and poop on a square of Astroturf in the bow. The Astroturf is then dumped into the water and trailed until clean.

Pets also get seasick, just like humans. Unlike humans, however, they seem to recover after a few hours. Having no watches to stand, they just curl up and sleep until the rough weather is over.

Although all of the pet owners realized that their pets were prone to seasickness occasionally, I found it surprising that few had thought to ask their home vet for emergency pet medical supplies, such as antibiotics. My experience has been that vets are always happy to suggest and prescribe a pet medical kit.

To my knowledge, every one of the cats had fallen overboard once. To their owners' amazement, they swam well.

Do you carry one or more bicycles?

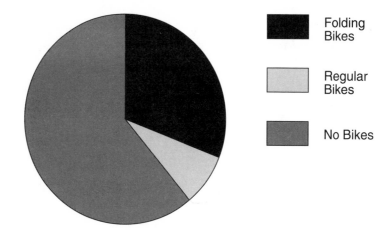

Folding Bikes

Regular Bikes

No Bikes

Thirty-nine percent of the boats carried bicycles. Three-quarters of these folded so they could be stored below, out of the corrosive salt atmosphere. Most of the non-folding bikes were of the police auction variety—cheap, rusty vehicles which could be replaced every year for $20.

The folding bikes were usually Dahons—beautifully engineered, three-speed, 16-inch-wheel machines that rode like full-size bikes, but folded into the volume of a medium-size suitcase. Their owners raved about them. Eighty percent of their owners felt they were worth the full $300 retail price, although discounts of 20% are common.

Do you regularly snorkel or SCUBA when you are in warm waters?

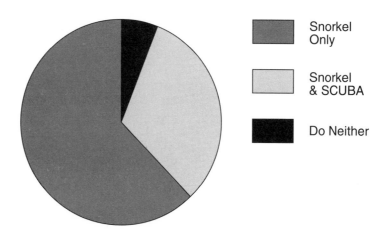

Snorkel Only

Snorkel & SCUBA

Do Neither

When cruising the Keys, the Bahamas, or the Caribbean, the water is 80°F and clear as tap water.

Ninety-four percent of the cruisers either snorkeled or SCUBA'd on a regular basis. Thirty-nine percent have a SCUBA license and use it. Another 5% have the license but find snorkeling satisfying enough.

Do you catch and eat fish on a regular basis?

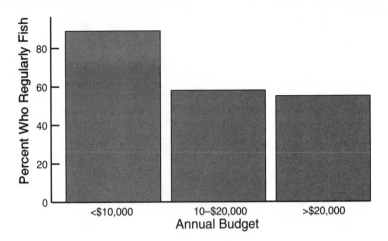

Overall, 73% catch fish by either diving or trolling while underway. The experience of eating fish fresher than any you can buy in a market is too delicious for any budget to pass up; however, the graph above demonstrates that fish are a staple for those on the smaller budgets.

14. Financial

Introduction

There is only one thing people are more secretive about than their intimate sex lives—their money. For this reason I stressed that none of their answers would be associated with either their name or the name of their boat. In fact, I didn't even ask their names. I also left the financial questions to the end of the survey.

This chapter contains both good and bad news.

First, the bad news. Unless you are a famous artist, author, or photographer, you will not be able to earn your way underway. I am a not-famous author with seven books in print, and I do all my writing on the boat; and yet, I am forced to stay in port next to a telephone and a P.O. box six months a year in order to go cruising for the other six.

Now, the good news. You can cruise full time on less than a poverty-level income. One-third of the cruisers interviewed were having a marvelous time on incomes so small they paid no taxes.

This chapter will tell you how long you can expect to go cruising on the income or equity you have.

Did you purchase your boat through a broker or direct from the owner?

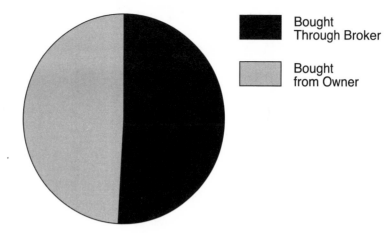

First, you have to buy a boat. Fifty-one percent purchased their boats through brokers, and 49% bought directly from previous owners.

What was the asking price, and what did you actually pay for your boat?

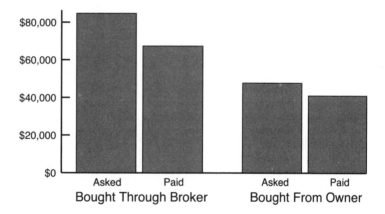

Prices asked and paid were far higher through brokers than from owners. This is not an indication that brokers are a more expensive way to shop, but that brokers handled more of the larger and more expensive boats.

The average asked price through brokers was $84,750. The corresponding average price paid was $67,350, or 79% of the listed price. Average boat size was 38.4 feet.

The average asked price from owners was $47,790. The average price paid was $41,060, or 86% of the asked price. Average boat size was 35.7 feet.

An analysis of asked versus paid prices (graph on next page) reveals an interesting psychology. Fifty percent of the cruisers paid about 95% of the prices being asked. In fact, 15% paid the full price. I didn't ask why, but one brazen soul had paid 102% of list!

paid versus asked prices

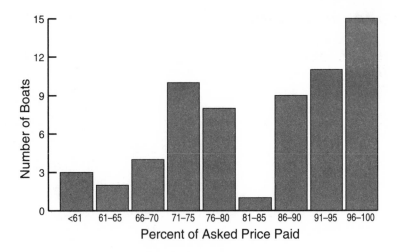

On the other hand, 35% had paid about three-quarters of the asked price; 7% had paid two-thirds; and one had paid only 40%.

There is a lesson to be learned here. If your psyche can take repeated rejection, and if you are willing to settle for something close to but not exactly your ideal, you can save tens of thousands of dollars on the purchase.

Two stories indicate the savings potential.

I have a friend who reasons that lots of well-off couples retire to Florida. The husband still nurtures the fantasy of sailing into the sunset, so he buys and equips the perfect cruising boat. Unfortunately, he has the dream and the money but not the health. He dies.

The widow, who knows little and cares less about boats, soon gets tired of dealing with the unpleasant reminder that is also deteriorating in the relentless Florida sun at an alarming rate. After a year on the market, she is primed for my friend. He offers her 50% of the asked price, flashes a green roll, and, one time in a hundred, she takes it.

The second story strikes closer to home. I knew the boat I was looking for. New, it sold for $167,500. When I saw a five-year-old one listed for $85,000, I put down a 10% nonrefundable deposit and bought it sight unseen.

Two years later I met a broker with this story. "Listed a boat just like yours. Spent hundreds of dollars advertising it in the sailing mags at $110,000. One day, before the ads had even appeared, the owner called me up and said to take it off the market. Someone had offered him $29,000 cash and he took it! Can you believe it!"

Excluding repairs and regular maintenance, how much have you spent on improvements and additional equipment for your boat?

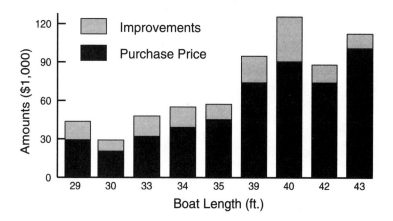

You'd be wise to budget a substantial amount for upgrades to your boat. Most boats have never been fully outfitted for extended cruising. Often the seller is changing boats and will take with him all of the gear not glassed in or welded down.

The average amount spent upgrading the boat after initial purchase was $17,620. That is one-third of the average purchase price of $54,390. Purchase and upgrade together add up to an average investment of $72,010.

Looking at investment versus boat length, two bargains stand out. First, there are more 30-footers than any other. Consequently, they flood the market and can be had relatively inexpensively.

Second, 42-foot boats are just longer than the ideal (according to the survey). There are also a lot of 42-footers retired from the Caribbean charter business. If you like boat maintenance, a 42-foot may be a bargain.

What percentage of your annual budget is derived from what financial source?

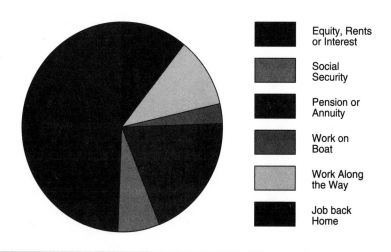

OK. Where's the money coming from? I and a few others had hopes of working our way around the world. I'm a writer with a laptop computer and should be able to write anywhere, including in the cockpit of a boat.

Others thought they'd take exotic photographs and sell them to slick magazines or calendar companies, or find a stash of native crafts and ship them home to the Haitian Art store on the corner.

What we all found, instead, was that selling anything, be it a book contract, a photo, or a crate of native art, requires communications. It requires a mailing address (not a mail drop from which you receive your mail after two or three weeks), a telephone, an answering machine, and possibly a fax.

The pie chart on the previous page shows where the cruisers were getting their money. Half was from equity, rents, and interest. Twenty percent came from retirement pensions or annuities, and another 7% from Social Security. Eleven percent was earned by periodically returning to a job at home, while a second 11% was earned at jobs along the way. Only 3% came from work performed aboard the boat.

What is your total annual budget, including all expenditures, except monthly boat payments?

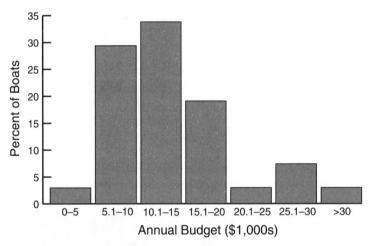

The most interesting question in the survey has to be, "What do you spend per year?"

The graph above shows the distribution of total annual budgets, including all costs, except boat payments. The figures do include boat insurance and maintenance.

The average for all boats was $13,987. Dividing by the average crew of 2.1, the annual cost per person was $6,600.

The graph shows that while it is difficult to cruise on less than $5,000, it is also difficult to spend over $20,000.

With the same boat, how little do you think you could live on and still make living aboard worthwhile?

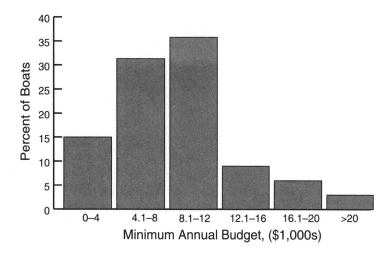

Minimum Annual Budget, ($1,000s)

Most of the cruisers seemed to be living quite well. They offered up cold Heinekens, Dewars Scotch, and cashews. So, I was interested in how much of their budgets were flab. I asked them how little they thought they could live on and still prefer cruising to returning to the real world.

On average, they felt they could cut their budgets by about a third. The average minimum budget was $9,094, or $4,330 per person.

In case this is still beyond your budget, those who had been to South and Central America said they had lived there on half of that!

What average cash kitty do you carry aboard?

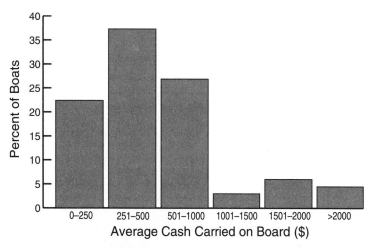

Average Cash Carried on Board ($)

Without an automobile and a checking account at a local bank, it is difficult to get your hands on cash (more on that later). The average amount of cash carried on board was $717—less in the U.S. and more abroad.

When the kitty runs out, how do you most often replenish it?

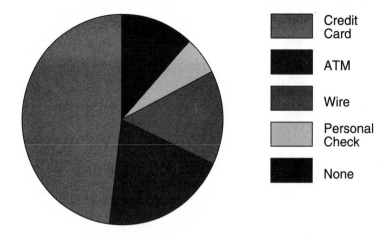

When the cash kitty runs dry, where do the cruisers turn to replenish the cookie jar? Forty-eight percent obtained cash advances on their credit cards. Twenty percent used automatic teller machines (ATMs), which are now found even in supermarkets. Fourteen percent had money wired to a local bank from their home bank. Only 6% found someone who would cash a personal check.

Several had a method for avoiding paying interest on the credit card advances. They would send a check in the same amount plus fees the very same day they obtained the advance.

ATMs are gaining rapidly in popularity. If you choose one of the larger systems (Plus, Cirrus, Most, etc.), chances are good that you will find one that speaks your language within walking distance wherever you anchor. And ask your banker for one of the little books that list all of the ATM locations for your system.

What credit card do you use most often?

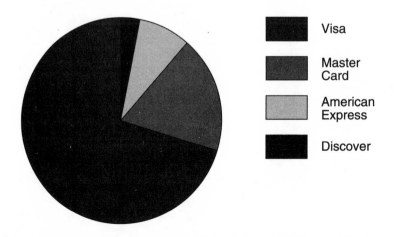

The average number of credit cards carried was three. The most popular, by far, was Visa. Some cruisers had half a dozen Visa cards. I was surprised at the small number of American Express cards.

Nearly everyone mentioned the value of having a "gold card." Whether American Express, Visa, or Master Card, the gold version usually covers rental car insurance at no cost.

Most cruisers rent automobiles several times per year to return home for the holidays and to do major provisionings. Without a gold card, it is maddening to rent a Florida car for $78 per week and then fork out another $77 for the collision damage waiver.

What is your average monthly phone bill?

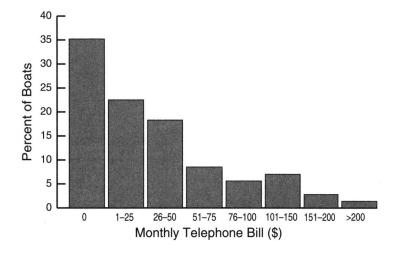

If you had a ham rig and appropriate license, you could hook up with a fellow ham in your hometown who would patch you through by phone to your loved ones for free. Unfortunately, only two of the cruisers I interviewed had the required "general license."

If you had a SSB, you could call the AT&T high seas operator and, for only *$5 per minute,* call people from your boat.

Within covered areas (generally within 20 miles of the coast from Bar Harbor, ME, to Miami, FL), you can use a cellular phone from your boat, just as you would from a car, but that's expensive, too.

Note that 35% have a phone bill of $0. They tell friends they'd love to stay in touch, but since it has to be by pay phone, it will have to be collect. A singlehander used this technique to update his little black book. When a girlfriend refused the call, he knew she had a new boyfriend!

For what percentage of its present fair market value is your boat insured?

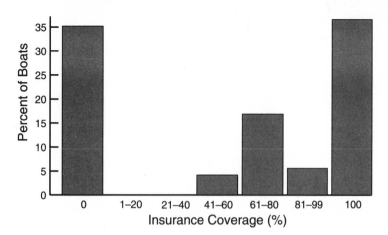

Hull insurance is one of the most expensive items in any cruiser's budget. For a standard, 1% deductible, East Coast of U.S. to 100 miles offshore policy, the cost runs around 1.5% of the face amount. Thus, a $100,000 policy would cost about $1,500 per year.

Small wonder then that 35% carried no boat insurance. A lot of the uninsured said they felt they were more competent than the occasional boater and didn't feel like subsidizing those who left their boats with open seacocks, didn't know where their through hulls were, and generally couldn't navigate their ways out of paper bags. For one year's premium, they could purchase ground tackle that would hold them through 100-mph winds.

Of the remaining 65% who did carry boat insurance, the average coverage was for 88% of the replacement value. Thirty-seven percent had 100% coverage, as required by the terms of their boat loans.

(U.S. boats only) Do you have medical insurance?

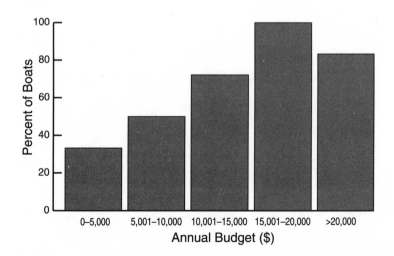

I was surprised to find that 65% (73% counting the Canadians) of the cruisers had medical insurance. This was invariably a carry-over feature of their retirement plans. Very few of those without pensions had or could afford the medical insurance commonly available to the self-employed or the unemployed.

The impact of income on ability to afford insurance is shown in the graph on the previous page. Only one in three of those living on $5,000 or less were covered, compared to 100% of those living on $15,000 to $20,000.

Appendix A: The Ideal Boat

There is no such thing as the ideal boat. Every boat represents compromise. If it sails well in light air, it probably doesn't in heavy. If it has a full keel and tracks well, then it will be hard to turn. If it sleeps a lot of people, then it probably has limited storage, and so on.

In spite of the above, I thought it useful to list all of the responses to the "What will your next . . . be?" questions. I asked the questions with reminders of the need to compromise. Typically, I would ask, "What water capacity would you like on this boat, bearing in mind that more water will slow the boat down?"

Here are the answers:

Question	Average Answer
Length on deck	39 feet 8 inches
Hull material	Fiberglass (75%)
Type of rig	Cutter (56%)
Roller furling jib	(85%)
Bimini awning	(93%)
Diesel power	43 hp
Fuel capacity	130 gallons
Range under power	1,222 nm
Battery capacity	520 Ah
Water capacity	175 gallons
Dinghy type	Inflatable (75%)
Dinghy material	Rubber (75%)

Appendix B: Four Budgets/Lifestyles

"What does it cost?" is the question cruisers most often hear from their landlocked brethren. Some who have never been there think there are cruisers living on coconut and fish and nothing else. Others, used to weekend sailing out of a marina, are convinced they couldn't live on less than what they now spend on land. The answer is that it *does* cost money, and that you'd better have a kitty put away or a steady flow of cash from a pension or investments. But the amount that it costs is probably less than you think.

The table below shows the sort of lifestyle you might expect on four different annual budgets, ranging from less than $10,000 to over $20,000. The annual budgets include all costs, except for boat payments and equipment upgrades. In other words, when planning your own lifestyle, either assume your boat is fully paid for and fully equipped or add estimated boat payments.

What is striking about the table is that most of the measures of lifestyle seem unrelated to budget. In fact, the cruisers with the least money seem to be having the best time!

Range of Annual Budget:	Less than $10,000	$10,000 to $14,999	$15,000 to $19,999	More than $20,000
Budget ($)	6,553	11,575	15,636	24,842
Boat length (ft.)	33.8	37.2	41.1	38.1
Age of boat (yr.)	20.3	10.5	14.1	9.4
Distance cruised (nm)	23,680	7,650	18,980	12,880
Dinghy outboard (hp)	4.1	6.3	6.8	6.5
Cruising life rating (1 to 10)	7.94	7.83	8.09	6.90
Stress compared to land, more	6%	10%	0%	16%
less	83%	60%	82%	53%
same	11%	30%	18%	31%
Restaurant dinner (nights/month)	3.9	2.8	3.3	4.5
Socialize w/ others (nights/month)	14.6	12.9	14.8	11.0
Monthly phone bill ($)	21	62	44	50
Have wind power	22%	30%	18%	32%
Have solar power	39%	10%	40%	16%
Have refrigeration	72%	60%	73%	90%
Have microwave	22%	20%	36%	16%
Have VCR	33%	40%	55%	58%
Percent boat insured	24%	73%	63%	73%
Have medical insurance	55%	75%	82%	95%

Appendix C: Saving Water

Getting potable water is difficult, except when purchasing diesel fuel. Since cruisers try to limit their use of expensive fuel, and since a boat can run many hundreds of miles on a tank of diesel, most boats run out of water before they run out of fuel.

For these reasons cruisers have learned a lot of tricks for the conservation of water. Practicing these extreme water-conservation tricks, my wife and I lived for 80 days in the Bahamas on just 90 gallons of water.

Bathing
Swim every day when you are in warm waters. It's the best exercise in the world, and it will keep you reasonably clean. I take a wash cloth in with me and remove the first layer of dirt, perspiration, and bacteria by vigorously rubbing every square inch of my body while in the water.

If you are not really dirty, but just sticky, try rubbing your body with a washcloth that has been saturated with a capful of hair conditioner or fabric softener. You'll be amazed at how clean you will feel. Of course, there is the old standby which your mother used to do for you when you were a baby—powder your skin just before turning in.

When the time comes when nothing but a bath will do, there are several variations on the "Navy shower."

The first is the classic version and should take no more than one gallon. Using a water-saving shower head, a solar shower, or a garden sprayer:

- wet your body all over, turn off the water, and then shampoo you hair;
- squeeze the lather from your hair and use it to soap the rest of your body;
- turn on the water and rinse from your head down.

The second version combines a saltwater wash with a freshwater rinse, and should take about half a gallon:

- jump in the water;
- exit the water and shampoo and lather your entire body with most any dishwashing detergent;
- jump in the water again and rinse all of the detergent from your hair and body;
- get out and rinse with fresh water or,
- get out, rinse hair only, and dry body immediately with a towel (one quart required).

Dish Washing

There is always the option of using paper plates and plastic forks, but most cruising cooks enjoy setting a fancy dinner table.

It's more efficient to wash a lot of dishes at once than to do them every time one is dirtied, so rinse them immediately in salt water and then store them in a deep sink or plastic tub until you've accumulated as many as you can handle at once.

You can also save water by saving dishes. Serve meals that can be prepared in a single pot. Stews, chowders and wok dishes are good examples.

Washing dishes is similar to washing your body. There are two popular versions of the Navy dish wash as well.

The first uses only fresh water and requires a prodigal two gallons:

- wash all of the dishes in one gallon of warm soapy water in a dishpan and stack so soap will drain;
- empty the wash water and refill the dishpan with fresh cool water;
- using a cup, rinse each dish over the dishpan, saving the rinse water for other cleaning tasks.

The second version uses only one quart of fresh water:

- wash all of the dishes in salt water and a detergent;
- rinse all of the dishes in salt water;
- immediately after rinsing, dry each dish with a dishtowel to remove both water and salt;
- soak the dishtowel in fresh water, wring hard to remove the brackish water, and dry in the sun.

Clothes Washing

If you are cruising full time, you should be in a warm, sunny climate all year long. That being the case, trade in your old wardrobe for one based on the bathing suit.

In the Keys and Bahamas, many cruisers wear bathing suits except when dining out in a restaurant. If you have three or four suits, wear them in swimming once a day, and then let them dry in the sun, they will rarely require fresh water laundering. When they need laundering, wash them in salt water with a detergent.

Save your laundry until you see a rain cloud coming. Wash everything in a large bucket or dishpan full of salt water and a liquid detergent. Use a small old-fashioned washboard for scrubbing. Wring, then hang the clothes up to rinse in the rain.

Catching Rain

The amount of water that falls on the deck of a boat in a rainstorm is surprising. There are 7.5 gallons in one cubic foot, so each inch of rain amounts to $7.5 \div 12 = 0.625$ gallons per square foot of deck. My 39-foot boat has about 350 square feet of deck, so I could collect 220 gallons per inch of rain.

There are three good ways of collecting rain water.

1. If your boat has a raised bulwark and waterfills flush to the deck at a low point, you can let the rain wash the salt off the canvas and deck, then open the fills and stuff the scuppers. All of the water falling on the sails and deck will be trapped and flow into your tanks. Be sure *all* of the salt has been flushed away, however, or the whole tank will be brackish. It is also wise to use a filter, such as one leg of a pair of panty hose, inserted into the fill fitting.

2. Carry a polyethylene tarp that can be suspended horizontally under the boom. Install a plastic through hull with a hose adapter at the low point. If you keep the tarp clean, you can start collecting water immediately and feed it to the water tanks via the hose.

3. One cruiser installed a plastic through hull with hose adapter about one foot up from the foot of his sail. Now he can lower the sail two feet, hook up the hose, and collect rainwater while he is sailing.

Appendix D: Radio Communications

People on land have become dependent on the phone. Think of the people you know who have answering machines and portable phones in their homes and cellular phones in their automobiles. Boaters in marina slips can use home phones. If they stick close to shore, they can use their automobile cellular phones from their boats. But cruisers go far beyond the reach of wires and cellular stations. Their telephones are their marine radios.

Most of us watch the morning and evening news to get the latest weather forecast. Boaters do, too, when they are in a slip. But cruisers are often beyond the range of television signals. Again, they turn to their radios for the all-important weather information.

VHF Radios

VHF (Very High Frequency) transceivers can be used to talk to other boats up to about 20 nm, to land stations having high antennas to about 40 nm, and to the Coast Guard's very high and powerful transmitters to about 100 nm. Specific channels are designated for use in emergencies, establishing contact, and conversing with other vessels, land stations, bridge tenders, and the Coast Guard. Most units also receive the NOAA weather channels.

The table below lists VHF channels and their designated uses. Note that each channel is listed twice: 1) by channel number, and 2) by category of designated use.

VHF CHANNELS AND THEIR USES (NON-COMMERCIAL BOATS ONLY)

CH	Designated Use	Designated Use	CH
06	Navigation and safety between ships	Bridges and navigation between ships	13
09	Between non-commercial ships	Initial contact and emergencies	16
12	Port operations	Coast Guard	22
13	Bridges and navigation between ships	Navigation and safety between ships	06
14	Port operations	Marine telephone operator	24
16	Initial contact and emergencies	Marine telephone operator	25
20	Port operations	Marine telephone operator	26
22	Coast Guard	Marine telephone operator	27
24	Marine telephone operator	Marine telephone operator	28
25	Marine telephone operator	Marine telephone operator	84
26	Marine telephone operator	Marine telephone operator	85
27	Marine telephone operator	Marine telephone operator	86
28	Marine telephone operator	Marine telephone operator	87
65	Port operations	Between non-commercial ships	09
66	Port operations	Between non-commercial ships	68
68	Between non-commercial ships	Between non-commercial ships	69
69	Between non-commercial ships	Between non-commercial ships	71
71	Between non-commercial ships	Between non-commercial ships	72
72	Between non-commercial ships	Between non-commercial ships	78
73	Port operations	Port operations	12
74	Port operations	Port operations	14
78	Between non-commercial ships	Port operations	20
84	Marine telephone operator	Port operations	65
85	Marine telephone operator	Port operations	66
86	Marine telephone operator	Port operations	73
87	Marine telephone operator	Port operations	74

MF & HF Radios

MF & HF (Medium and High Frequency) radios are of three types. The least expensive are receive-only radios with which you can listen in on frequencies from 300 kHz to 30 MHz. More expensive are ham transceivers with which you can listen to all frequencies in the 300 kHz to 30 MHz range and transmit in the designated ham bands. The third and most expensive are marine SSB (single sideband) transceivers with which you can receive on all frequencies and transmit on the officially designated marine SSB frequencies.

The tables below list frequencies, modes, call signs, and times of transmissions I picked up from the cruisers who had such radios.

OFFSHORE VOICE WEATHER

GMT	EST	EDST	Sign	Location	Mode	Frequencies (kHz)			
0200	2100	2200	WAH	St. Thomas	USB	4357.4	4382.2	8728.2	13100.8
0400	2300	2400	NMN	Portsmouth	USB	4426.0	6501.0	8764.0	
1000	0500	0600	NMN	Portsmouth	USB	4426.0	6501.0	8764.0	
1000	0500	0600	WAH	St. Thomas	USB	4357.4	4382.2	8728.2	13100.8
1055	0555	0655	ANT	Antigua	AM	930.0			
1110	0610	0710	WOSO	San Juan	AM	1030.0			
1110	0610	0710	WVWI	St. Thomas	AM	1000.0			
1145	0645	0745	hams	Waterway Net	LSB	7268.0			
1155	0655	0755	BON	Bonaire	AM	800.0			
1155	0655	0755	WVWI	St. Thomas	AM	1000.0			
1200	0700	0800	WLO	Mobile	USB	4369.8	8808.8	17356.9	
1230	0730	0830	WVWI	St. Thomas	AM	1000.0			
1300	0800	0900	WOM	Ft. Lauderdale	USB	4363.6	8722.0		
1300	0800	0900	WVCG	Ft. Lauderdale	AM	1080.0			
1600	1100	1200	NMN	Portsmouth	USB	6501.0	8764.0	13089.0	
1800	1300	1400	WAH	St. Thomas	USB	4357.4	4382.2	8728.2	13100.8
2200	1700	1800	NMN	Portsmouth	USB	6501.0	8764.0	13089.0	
2220	1720	1820	ANT	Antigua	AM	930.0			
2300	180	1900	WOM	Ft. Lauderdale	USB	8722.0			

OFFSHORE NEWS

GMT	EST	EDST	Mode	Sign	Frequencies (kHz)			
0000	1900	2000	AM	BBC	6175.0	7325.0	9590.0	
0010	1910	2010	AM	BBC	5975.0	6195.0	11775.0	15215.0
0010	1910	2010	AM	VOA	5995.0	6130.0	9450.0	11695.0
0100	2000	2100	AM	VOA	5995.0			
1000	0500	0600	AM	BBC	9590.0			
1000	·0500	0600	AM	VOA	6030.0	6165.0		
1100	0600	0700	AM	BBC	6195.0	9590.0		
1100	0600	0700	AM	VOA	6030.0	6165.0		
1200	0700	0800	AM	BBC	6195.0			
1300	0800	0900	AM	BBC	6195.0			
2000	1500	1600	AM	BBC	5975.0	6175.0	6195.0	
2100	1600	1700	AM	BBC	5975.0	9915.0		
2220	1720	1820	AM	BBC	5975.0	6195.0	9915.0	

WEATHERFAX TRANSMISSIONS

GMT	EST	EDST	Fax Information

Halifax, NS — Western North Atlantic
USB: 6328.1, 10534.1, 13508.1 kHz

GMT	EST	EDST	Fax Information
0001	1901	2001	Significant weather
0015	1915	2015	Ice chart
0312	2212	2312	Surface analysis
0401	2301	0001	Wave analysis
0414	2314	0014	12-hr wave analysis
0514	0014	0114	24-hr wave analysis
0601	0101	0201	Significant weather
0614	0114	0214	36-hr wave analysis
0901	0401	0501	Surface analysis
1101	0601	0701	Ice chart
1201	0701	0801	Significant weather
1512	1012	1112	Surface analysis
1601	1101	1201	Wave analysis
1614	1114	1214	12-hr wave analysis
1714	1214	1314	24-hr wave analysis
1801	1301	1401	Significant weather
1814	1314	1414	36-hr wave analysis
2120	1620	1720	Surface analysis
2201	1701	1801	Ice chart

Boston, MA — N of 35°N & W of 60°W
USB: 3240.1, 7528.1 kHz

GMT	EST	EDST	Fax Information
0530	0030	0130	Surface analysis
0540	0040	0140	12-hr prognosis
0550	0050	0150	36-hr prognosis
0600	0100	0200	3 & 4-day prognosis
1730	1230	1330	Surface analysis
1740	1240	1340	24-hr prognosis
1750	1250	1350	48-hr prognosis
1800	1300	1400	Oceanographic analysis

Norfolk, VA — North Atlantic Ocean
USB: 3355.1, 8078.1, 10863.1 kHz

GMT	EST	EDST	Fax Information
0000	1900	2000	Schedule for next 24 hrs.

Mobile, AL — Gulf of Mexico
USB: 6850.1, 9156.6, 11143.1 kHz

GMT	EST	EDST	Fax Information
0250	2150	2250	Surface analysis
0300	2200	2300	Significant weather
0310	2210	2310	Offshore forecast
0850	0350	0450	Surface analysis
0900	0400	0500	Significant weather
0910	0410	0510	18/36-hr forecast
1450	0950	1050	Surface analysis
1500	1000	1100	Significant weather
1510	1010	1110	Offshore forecast
2030	1530	1630	Surface analysis
2040	1540	1640	Significant weather
2050	1550	1650	18/36-hr forecast

AT&T HIGH SEAS OPERATORS

Channel	Transmit (kHz)	Receive (kHz)

CFH — Halifax, NS

Channel	Transmit (kHz)	Receive (kHz)
403	4069.2	4363.6
602	6203.1	6509.5
810	8222.9	8746.8
1129	12416.8	13187.6
1607	16478.6	17251.5
2202	22003.1	22599.1

WOO — Manahawkin, NJ

Channel	Transmit (kHz)	Receive (kHz)
410	4090.9	4385.3
808	8216.7	8740.6
1203	12336.2	13107.0
1605	16472.4	17245.3
2201	22000.0	22596.0

WOM — Ft Lauderdale, FL

Channel	Transmit (kHz)	Receive (kHz)
403	4069.2	4363.6
802	8198.1	8722.0
1206	12345.5	13116.3
1601	16460.0	17232.9
2215	22043.4	22642.5

WLO — Mobile, AL

Channel	Transmit (kHz)	Receive (kHz)
405	4075.4	4369.8
824	8266.3	8790.2
1212	12364.1	13134.9
1641	16584.0	17356.9
2237	22111.6	22707.6

WAH — St. Thomas, VI

Channel	Transmit (kHz)	Receive (kHz)
401	4063.0	4357.4
604	6209.3	6515.7
804	8204.3	8728.2
1201	12330.0	13100.8
1602	16463.1	17236.0
2223	22068.2	22664.2

COAST GUARD EMERGENCY CALLS

Channel	Transmit (kHz)	Receive (kHz)
—	2182.0	2182.0
—	2670.0	2670.0
424	4134.3	4428.7
601	6200.0	6506.4
816	8241.5	8765.4
1205	12342.4	13113.2
1625	16534.4	17307.3

SHIP TO SHIP SSB (USB)

SSB Channel	Transmit/ Receive (kHz)	For Distance
—	2638.0	<50 nm
—	2738.0	<50 nm
4A	4125.0	>50 nm
4B	4146.0	>50 nm
4C	4149.0	>50 nm
6A	6224.0	>150 nm
6B	6227.0	>150 nm
6C	6230.0	>150 nm
8A	8294.0	>400 nm
8B	8297.0	>400 nm
8C	8300.0	>400 nm
12A	12353.0	>1000 nm
12B	12356.0	>1000 nm
12C	12359.0	>1000 nm

WWV TIME SIGNALS (AM)

5,000; 10,000; 15,000; 20,000 kHz

HAM NETWORKING

Frequency	Mode	Purpose
6215.0	USB	Hailing
7268.0	LSB	Waterway Net
21400.0	USB	Atlantic Maritime Net (1300–1400)
27530.0	USB	Maritime Mobile Net

Appendix E: Spring and Fall Migrations

Many cruisers migrate south in the fall and back north again in the spring in order to remain in eternal summer. The recommended departure dates on the various legs of the trip are shown in the chart below. The ranges of best dates are determined not only by seasonal temperatures, but by prevailing winds and the probabilities of storms as well.

For short coastal or ICW trips, hurricanes are of no more concern than usual. Long offshore passages, such as to and from Bermuda, however, should not be attempted before the end of the hurricane season—roughly November 1.

On the chart, "NR" means direct passage between two points is not recommended. Instead, one should make shorter trips which are both safer and more comfortable. For example, it is not recommended that one attempt to sail directly from Norfolk, VA, to the Bahamas, since this would entail rounding treacherous Cape Hatteras and bucking the Gulf Stream if one got too far offshore. It would be better to take the ICW (with short outside trips) to either Beaufort, NC, or to South Florida before crossing the Gulf Stream.

Similarly, in going from New England to the Bahamas, intermediate stops are recommended at Norfolk, Beaufort, and South Florida. Of course, most cruisers prefer to make only 40 to 60 nautical miles per day and enjoy the scenery and ports along the way.

Recommended Departure Dates

TO / FROM	New England	Norfolk VA	Beaufort NC	Bermuda	South Florida	Bahamas	U.S. Virgin Islands
New England		Sept 15 Oct 15	NR	Nov 1 Dec 1	NR	NR	Nov 1 Dec 1
Norfolk VA	June 1 July 1		Oct 15 Nov 15	Nov 1 Dec 1	NR	NR	Nov 1 Dec 1
Beaufort NC	NR	May 15 June 15		Nov 1 Dec 1	Nov 1 Dec 1	Nov 1 Dec 1	Nov 1 Dec 1
Bermuda	May 1 June 15	May 1 June 15	May 1 June 15		NR	Nov 1 May 1	Nov 1 Dec 15
South Florida	NR	NR	NR	NR		Nov 1 May 1	Nov 1 Dec 15
Bahamas	NR	NR	April 1 June 1	May 1 June 1	April 1 May 1		Nov 1 Dec 15
U.S. Virgin Islands	April 15 June 1	April 15 June 1	April 15 June 1	April 15 June 1	April 15 June 1	April 15 June 1	

Locations of Temperature Charts

The following pages contain charts displaying the average daily high and low temperatures for each month of the year at the 32 cruising destinations on the map below.

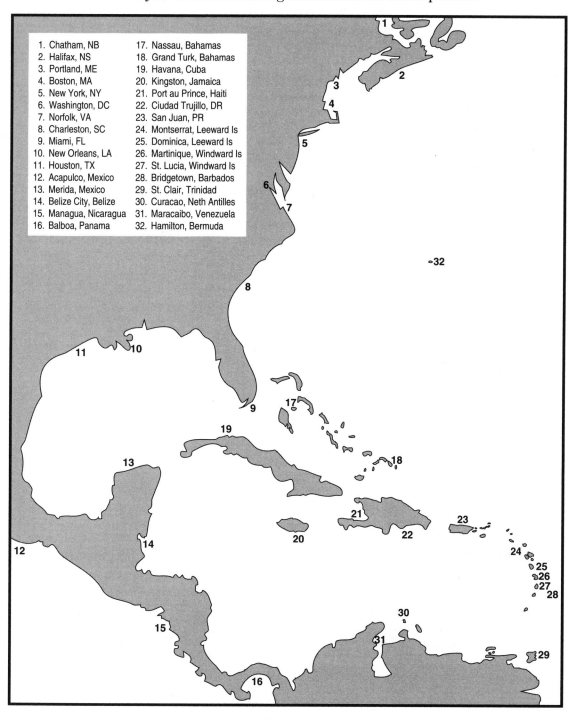

1. Chatham, NB
2. Halifax, NS
3. Portland, ME
4. Boston, MA
5. New York, NY
6. Washington, DC
7. Norfolk, VA
8. Charleston, SC
9. Miami, FL
10. New Orleans, LA
11. Houston, TX
12. Acapulco, Mexico
13. Merida, Mexico
14. Belize City, Belize
15. Managua, Nicaragua
16. Balboa, Panama
17. Nassau, Bahamas
18. Grand Turk, Bahamas
19. Havana, Cuba
20. Kingston, Jamaica
21. Port au Prince, Haiti
22. Ciudad Trujillo, DR
23. San Juan, PR
24. Montserrat, Leeward Is
25. Dominica, Leeward Is
26. Martinique, Windward Is
27. St. Lucia, Windward Is
28. Bridgetown, Barbados
29. St. Clair, Trinidad
30. Curacao, Neth Antilles
31. Maracaibo, Venezuela
32. Hamilton, Bermuda

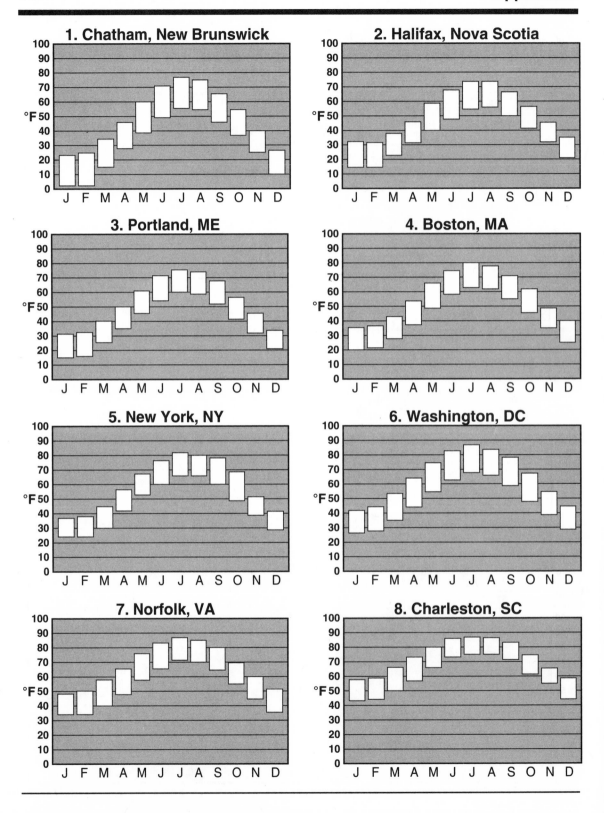

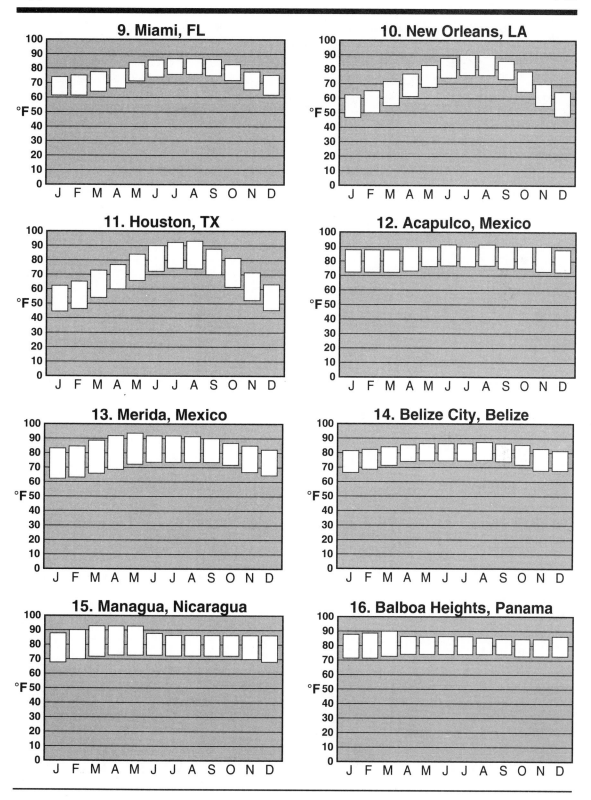

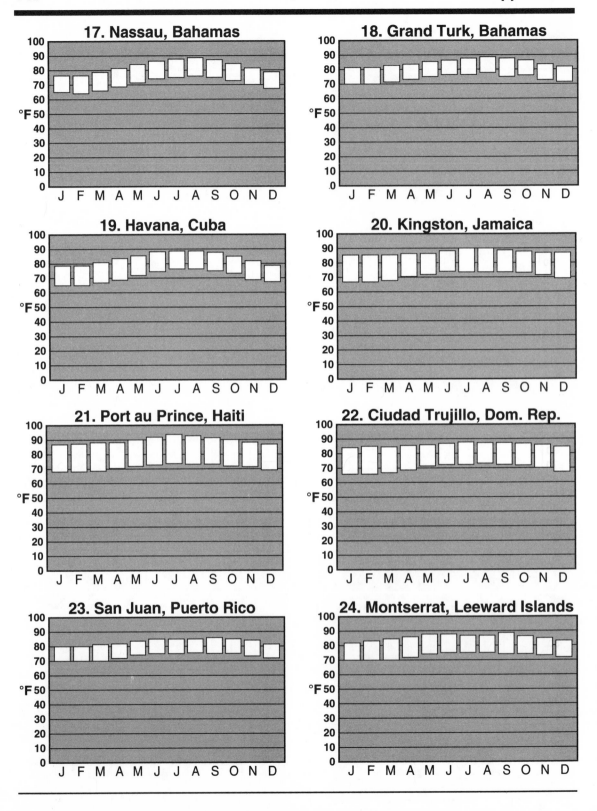

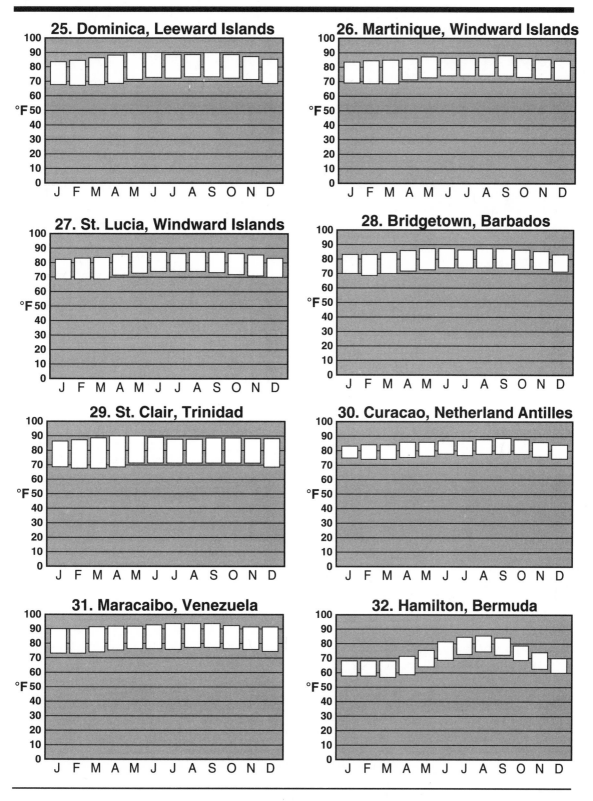

25. Dominica, Leeward Islands

26. Martinique, Windward Islands

27. St. Lucia, Windward Islands

28. Bridgetown, Barbados

29. St. Clair, Trinidad

30. Curacao, Netherland Antilles

31. Maracaibo, Venezuela

32. Hamilton, Bermuda

Glossary

Ah: amperes of current, times hours current is flowing.

Alternator: device that runs off engine power and produces direct current for running lights and charging batteries; differs from generator in that its field magnets rotate.

Ampere (Amp): measure of electric current.

Angle-of-Attack: angle at which wind strikes a sail.

Autopilot: electro-mechanical device for automatically steering a vessel.

Awning: canvas that shades an area of boat, usually the cockpit.

Bahamian Moor: method of anchoring in which two anchors are set from the bow in opposite directions.

Battery Bank: a set (may be one) of batteries, usually connected to give 12 volts.

Bilge: area inside a boat beneath the floor.

Bilge Pump: a pump, either manual or electric, for pumping accumulated water from the bilge.

Bimini: cockpit awning stretched on a pipe frame.

Bosun's Chair: canvas chair for hoisting a person up the mast.

Bowsprit: spar or other projection of the bow beyond the hull.

Bruce™ Anchor: one-piece cast anchor, resembling a shovel with its handle bent backward.

Cabin Heater: heater separate from the galley stove whose fumes are vented to the outside.

Cat: catboat rig—a single sail on a single mast.

Celestial Navigation: method of finding one's position on earth relative to the known positions of celestial bodies.

Cellular Phone: a radio-telephone system in which mobile telephones connect with fixed transceivers in overlapping cells or areas.

Centerboard: a board that is lowered from the center of the keel to increase the depth of the keel.

Cockpit: depressed area in the deck from which the boat is steered.

Condenser: heat exchanger in which the hot gaseous refrigerant is cooled and condensed to its liquid state.

Coordinates: latitude and longitude of a position on the earth.

Cutless Bearing: rubber shaft support that acts like a water-lubricated bearing forward of the propeller.

Cutter: sailing rig with a mainsail, two jibs, and a mainmast that is farther aft than on a sloop.

Danforth™ Anchor: lightweight anchor with two large trapezoidal flukes.

Davits: frames for raising and holding a dinghy out of the water; on a small boat they are usually at the stern.

Delivery: transporting a boat for the owner.

Depth Sounder: electronic device that bounces sound waves off the bottom to determine depth.

Desalinator: device for removing salt from water.

Dinghy: small boat for getting to and from a larger boat.

Displacement: 1) the weight of an unloaded boat, or 2) an estimate of the cargo-carrying capacity of a boat.

Displacement Boat: a boat that is too heavy to achieve planing speed.

Dockline: lines (nautical ropes) for securing a boat to a dock.

Dodger: structure at forward end of cockpit for protection of companionway from spray; usually made of canvas and tubing.

Draft: maximum projection below the waterline.

Drogue: anything dragged behind a boat to keep either bow or stern pointed into the wind in a storm.

Engine Mounts: rubber and steel feet that connect the engine to the hull.

EPIRB: Emergency Position Indicating Radio Beacon.

Evaporator: heat ex-changer inside a refrigerator that evaporates liquid refrigerant and absorbs heat.

Fathometer: same as depth sounder.

Fender: an object, usually inflated, hung between the hull and the dock to protect the finish of the boat.

Fender Board: board hung between fenders and vertical piles of a dock to provide protection of the topsides.

Ferrocement: hull material consisting of cement, sprayed over and reinforced by steel mesh.

Fiberglass: fiberglass reinforced plastic (FRP), the most popular material for small boat hulls.

Fisherman Anchor: classic anchor in which the arms are at right angles to the flukes.

Fish Finder: depth sounder that displays a continuous record of depth as well as intervening fish.

Fluke: flat blades of anchor that dig into the sea bottom.

Fortress™ Anchor: anchor that is similar to the "Danforth" anchor in shape, but made of aluminum.

Gasket (engine): material for sealing unmoving engine parts against leaks.

Gelcoat: pigmented resin applied over fiberglass structure as a finish.

Generator: device that runs off a small auxiliary engine and generates 110-volt AC and/or 12-volt DC power.

GPS: Global Positioning System—radio navigation system that finds continuous position by computing range to three or more satellites.

Grounding: going aground.

Ground Tackle: anchors and anchor rodes.

Halogen Light: efficient, high-intensity lamp filled with a halogen gas.

Halyard: line for raising sail.

Ham Radio: radio transceiver that operates only in the designated amateur radio bands.

Harness: web straps around the chest for attaching crewmember to a safety line.

Hatch: ventilation or access hole in deck which can be securely closed.

Hawse Pipe: pipe leading from deck to anchor locker.

Head: bathroom on a boat; also boat toilet.

Heading: direction a boat's bow is facing.

HF Radio: high frequency radio (up to 30 MHz).

Holding Tank: tank for holding head waste.

Hull/Deck Joint: mechanical joint where the hull and the deck are fastened.

Hull Speed: theoretical speed at which the length of the wave created by a boat's motion equals the boat's waterline length.

ICW: Intracoastal Waterway that runs along the Atlantic and Gulf Coasts.

Impeller: rotating blades of a circulation pump.

Injector: valve that sprays diesel fuel into the cylinder of a diesel engine.

Inverter: electrical device which converts DC power to AC power.

Jerrican: container for carrying fuel—usually of five-gallon capacity.

Jib: triangular sail hoisted on a forestay.

Kedge Off: using an anchor to pull a grounded boat into deeper water.

Ketch: sailboat having a mainmast and a mizzenmast located forward of the rudderpost.

Knockdown: sailing accident wherein a sailboat is heeled 90° by a sudden gust of wind.

Knot: a speed of one nautical mile per hour.

Length on Deck (LOD): length of the deck of a boat, not including bowsprit or pulpit.

Length Overall (LOA): maximum length of a boat, including all forward and aft projections.

Leeward: downwind, or the direction toward which the wind is blowing.

Liferaft: inflatable platform designed to protect crew of a sunken ship from the elements.

Lifesling: patented device for retrieving a person from the water.

Line: any rope on a boat.

Loran: Long Range Aid to Navigation—a radio navigation device which finds position by comparing time delays of signals from a master and two slave transmitters.

Magnetic Course: direction of a ship's course expressed as degrees clockwise from the direction of magnetic north (direction a compass points).

Mail Drop: temporary address at which mail is collected for cruisers.

Mainsail: sail whose luff is fastened to the mainmast.

Manual Pump: hand- or foot-operated pump.

Mast Steps: steps fastened to the mast for climbing.

Mizzenmast: small mast aft of the mainmast.

MOB: man overboard.

Mooring: permanent anchoring system for a boat.

Motorboat: boat whose only means of propulsion is by engine.

Motorsailer: boat which combines the characteristics of a sailboat and a motorboat.

MTBF: mean time between failures.

Nautical Mile: 6,076 feet, or 1.15 statute miles.

Navigation Station: place on boat where navigation is performed.

Overall Length: same as Length Overall.

Packing Nut: nut designed to compress a packing material around a rotating shaft to prevent leakage of fluids.

Passage: trip over water with no stops.

Passagemaking: doing a passage.

PFD: personal flotation device—life jacket.

Pile: piling, or vertical pole, driven into the sea bottom for docking.

Pilothouse: rigid structure enclosing steering station.

Piloting: the art of safely navigating a vessel.

Plow Anchor: steel anchor resembling a double-sided garden plow.

Port(hole): window in side of boat for view, light, and ventilation. If non-opening, it would be called a portlight.

Pressure Pump: motor-driven pump for delivering fluids under pressure.

Purge Air: remove air from a fluid-filled line.

Rail: top edge of the hull/deck joint. Also, horizontal pipes supported by vertical stanchions to prevent people from falling overboard.

RDF: radio direction finder—electronic device for finding the direction to a radio transmitter.

Reef: to temporarily reduce the area of a sail.

Rig: style of boat determined by sizes and arrangement of sails.

Rigging: masts, booms, stays, shrouds, and lines used to control sails.

Rode: anchor line, including chain.

Roller Furling Reefing: reefing by rolling up the sail.

Rudderpost: shaft that supports the rudder.

Running Rigging: all of the moving lines and hardware for raising and controlling sails.

Safety Harness: same as harness.

Sailboat: a boat whose primary propulsion is by sail.

Satellite Navigator (Sat-nav): electronic navigation device that determines position by measuring the shift in frequency transmitted by a passing satellite.

Schooner: sailing rig with at least two masts, the aft-most being the same height or taller than the others.

Scope: ratio of rode out to the vertical distance from the sea bottom to the point of attachment to the boat.

SCUBA: self-contained underwater breathing apparatus.

Sea Anchor: apparatus towed behind a boat in a storm in order to hold the bow into the wind.

Seacock: through-hull valve that can be closed.

Seal (engine): material surrounding a rotating shaft on an engine to prevent loss of fluids.

Set (anchor): make the anchor dig into the bottom.

Shaft: the rod which connects the propeller to the output of the engine or transmission.

Sheet: line for controlling the free corner of a sail.

Shroud: wire that braces the mast in the transverse (abeam) direction.

Singlehander: a person operating a vessel alone.

Siphon: phenomenon by which water apparently defies gravity by flowing from a higher to a lower point through a pipe that rises above the water level.

Sloop: sail rig with a mainsail and a single jib.

Spar: mast, boom, or gaff.

Spinnaker: parachute-like sail that is flown downwind.

Spreader: horizontal members which, together with the shrouds, brace a mast when under sail.

SSB: single-sideband radio, used for communicating long distances.

Standing Rigging: the non-moving parts of a rig.

Statute Mile: 5,280 feet, or 0.869 nautical mile.

Stay: wire that braces a mast in the fore and aft direction.

Steering Post: vertical rod about which the rudder pivots—same as rudder post.

Storm Sail: small sail used when sailing in storm conditions.

Stuffing Box: shaft seal that allows shaft to rotate without leaking.

Tell-Tale: light string or ribbon that shows the direction of the wind.

Through Hull: a penetration of the hull.

Topsides: area of the hull above the waterline.

Transmission: mechanical device between the engine and the propeller shaft for changing the speed and/or direction of shaft rotation.

Transom: transverse area of a boat's stern.

Trawler: displacement type of fishing boat designed to tow nets, or pleasure cruiser that resembles same.

True Course: the direction of a boat's line of travel relative to geographic or true north.

VHF: very-high frequency radio used for communicating short distances.

Waypoint: a predetermined position or checkpoint along a planned course—the course direction usually changes at waypoints.

Weatherfax: facsimile machine designed to receive and print weather charts.

Winch: geared mechanical device for tightening running rigging.

Wind Generator: wind-driven electric generator or alternator.

Windlass: geared mechanical device for raising an anchor.

Wind Vane: mechanical device that automatically steers a boat at a constant angle relative to the wind.

Windward: upwind, or in the direction from which the wind is blowing.

WWV Time Signals: audible time signals broadcast by radio station WWV for synchronizing clocks to Universal Coordinated Time, formerly known as Greenwich Mean Time (GMT).

Yawl: sailing rig with a mainmast forward and a mizzenmast aft of the rudderpost.

Index